John Grier Hibben

The Problems of Philosophy

An introduction to the study of philosophy

John Grier Hibben

The Problems of Philosophy
An introduction to the study of philosophy

ISBN/EAN: 9783337070687

Printed in Europe, USA, Canada, Australia, Japan

Cover: Foto ©Paul-Georg Meister /pixelio.de

More available books at **www.hansebooks.com**

THE PROBLEMS OF PHILOSOPHY

AN INTRODUCTION TO THE STUDY OF PHILOSOPHY

BY

JOHN GRIER HIBBEN, Ph.D.
STUART PROFESSOR OF LOGIC IN PRINCETON
UNIVERSITY

CHARLES SCRIBNER'S SONS
NEW YORK   CHICAGO   BOSTON

PREFACE

It has been my aim in this work to give a simple statement of the various schools of philosophy, with the salient features of their teachings, and to indicate the chief points at issue in reference to controverted questions. There has been no attempt to present a detailed account or exhaustive criticism of philosophical systems; but merely to furnish the student who is beginning the study of philosophy a bird's-eye view of the general philosophical territory. It is my earnest hope that from these cursory glimpses he may be led to a more extended and serious exploration.

One who is undertaking for the first time a course in the history of philosophy finds himself naturally at a loss to understand the relations between earlier and later periods of thought, and therefore wants a proper perspective; accordingly he fails to appreciate the drift of things. To all such an introduction to the main problems, and general tendencies of philosophical discussion, should prove an invaluable assistance in interpreting the evolution of thought historically.

I have tried to define the many technical terms in such a manner as to acquaint the reader with the language of philosophy, and yet at the same time to avoid the use of such terms as far as possible in explaining the distinctive doctrines of the different philosophical schools.

J. G. H.

REDFIELD, NEW YORK,
August 8, 1898.

CONTENTS

CHAPTER		PAGE
I.	A Plea for Philosophy	1
II.	The Problems of Philosophy	14
III.	The Problem of Being ("Ontology")	32
IV.	The World Problem ("Cosmology")	59
V.	The Problem of Mind ("Psychology")	78
VI.	The Problem of Knowledge ("Epistemology")	95
VII.	The Problem of Reason ("Logic")	118
VIII.	The Problem of Conscience ("Ethics")	134
IX.	The Problem of Political Obligation ("Political Science")	158
X.	The Problem of the Sense of Beauty ("Æsthetics")	181
	Index	199

THE PROBLEMS OF PHILOSOPHY

CHAPTER I

A PLEA FOR PHILOSOPHY

THERE is in the minds of some, perhaps of many, a false conception of philosophy. The popular verdict would agree no doubt with Keats:—

> "Do not all charms fly
> At the mere touch of cold philosophy."

From the days when Socrates, to the delight of the Athenian audience, was exposed to the good-natured banter of Aristophanes, the philosopher has ever been regarded as a visionary creature, essentially unpractical in his point of view, repudiating common-sense judgments, his head in the clouds, his feet spurning the earth.

When Thales fell into a well, as he walked and gazed at the stars, a witty Thracian maiden remarked that he was so eager to know what was going on in heaven, that he could not see what was before his feet. And it is true that many have followed in Thales' footsteps.

Even a more thoughtful reflection may still leave the impression that the philosopher, after long years of patient introspection and persevering research, fails at last to contribute permanently to the world's thought, or materially to further its progress. The scientist, the inventor, the statesman, the man of affairs, leave behind them visible and tangible results which make for prosperity, and health, and a more abounding life. But of philosophy, it is urged, in the words of Bacon, that "like a virgin consecrated to God, she bears no fruit." Even among those who would not assent wholly to this stricture upon philosophy, there still lingers the feeling that there is grave danger lest philosophic inquiry degenerate into barren disputation. No one could have had a higher ideal of the offices of a true philosopher than Lotze, and yet this same feeling was no doubt in his mind when he said: "The continual sharpening of the knife becomes tiresome if, after all, we have nothing to cut with it."

A philosopher, however, is not fairly judged by his eccentricities, nor by the frailties to which he is liable; still less should his philosophy as a whole fall into ill-repute because of those among its devotees who have stumbled into wells, or who aimlessly pass their lives in whetting their faculties and then neglecting to use them. The problems of philosophy are, in fact, the problems of life, the burden and the mystery of existence, the origin and destiny of man, the relations which he sustains to the world of which he is a part, and to the unseen universe which lies round about him. Though they may not be couched in philosophical language, such questionings of heart and of mind we cannot wholly silence. For, when we are most deeply engrossed in the everyday round of work and worry, and when the problems of life seem to narrow down to the problem of the ways and means of bare existence, then, —

> "There's a sunset-touch
> A fancy from a flower-bell, some one's death
> A chorus-ending from Euripides, —
> And that's enough for fifty hopes, and fears
> As old and new at once as Nature's self."

In the face of the good-natured gibe or the ill-natured sneer, man is a philosopher in spite of himself. It must be allowed, nevertheless, that while there is a philosophy which is spontaneous, vital, and productive, there is also a philosophy which is inert and barren. Much that is called discussion is a mere raising of the dust which obscures the vision and irritates the disposition. Goethe, himself a philosopher as well as a poet, has quite roundly abused a speculative spirit of this kind in the sneer of Mephistopheles: —

> "Ich sag' es dir; ein Kerl der speculirt,
> Ist wie ein Thier, auf dürrer Heide
> Von einem bösen Geist im Kreis geführt
> Und rings umher liegt schöne grüne Weide."

And yet Goethe would have been the first to defend that sort of speculation which is characterized by an open mind, an earnest spirit of inquiry, and a love of the truth which draws living water from the deep springs of reality.

Plato describes philosophers as lovers of the truth, of that which *is*, — impassioned lovers. This is the most satisfactory as well as the simplest definition of the philosopher. He is a lover of that which *is*, in distinction from that which seems to be. He seeks a reason for the phenomena of existence; he is not satisfied with a mere description of their mode of behavior, or with a mere formulation of the laws which express the causal relation of these phenomena. The problem of philosophy differs from the problem of science. It is the problem of science, as John Stuart Mill puts it, "to discover what are the fewest number of phenomenal data which, being granted, will explain the phenomena of experience." Philosophy probes deeper. It seeks to reveal also the *raison d'être* of these fundamental data, and their relation to the thinking self which observes them, and reasons about them, as well as their relation to the power which constitutes and directs their elemental energy. The philosopher should be the "synoptic" man, one who sees the verities of life in their true relations, properly coördinated or subordinated, and who, in particular pursuits, however absorbing, does not ignore the unity of the whole, nor overlook the universal aspect even of the commonplaces of life.

The philosopher and poet here meet on common ground. Each strives to apprehend the reality which underlies appearance, to discover the "open secret of the world." To appreciate the wealth of philosophy's contribution to the thought of humanity, we must not forget that, shorn of their technical terminology, and translated into the living words and flaming symbols of poetry, philosophical ideas have appealed to innumerable minds for whom formal philosophy must have remained forever a sealed book. The poet naturally commands a larger audience than the philosopher, because of the form in which he casts his thought, and, yet, he is truly a philosopher, — so far as he is a true poet, meditating upon the deep things of God, and hymning his song "on man, on nature, and on human life." The poet, as well as the philosopher, sees in the world in which he lives far more than the fleeting panorama of events, and the surface show of things. We may take the closing lines of Kipling's "L'Envoi," as a just expression of the ideal of the poet's life and work: —

"And only the Master shall praise us, and only the
    Master shall blame;
And no one shall work for money, and no one
    shall work for fame;
But each for the joy of the working, and each in
    his separate star,
Shall draw the thing as he sees it for the God of
    things as they are."

Deprive poetry of this which it has in common with philosophy, — the seeing of things as they are, — and the beauty and fragrance of the flower are gone. The blending of philosophy and poetry appears in consummate excellence in Tennyson's "In Memoriam." The following quotation from Tennyson's biography will serve to illustrate this somewhat at length: —

"Men like Maurice and Robertson thought that the author of 'In Memoriam' had made a definite step towards the unification of the highest religion and philosophy with the progressive science of the day; and that he was the one poet who, 'through almost the agonies of a death-struggle,' had made an effective stand against his own doubts and difficulties, and those of the time 'on behalf of those first principles which underlie all creeds, which belong to our earliest childhood, and on which the wisest and best have rested through all ages.'"[1] It is this all-embracing vision which constitutes the poetic insight, and the philosophic insight as well. Though the poet may experience less sombre moods than those which seem to bring him to the

[1] Vol. I, p. 298.

"agonies of a death-struggle" and may strike his lyre with lighter touch, still, his deeper themes are no less susceptible of a harmonious expression, and the chords of his thought stir and soothe as the more joyous strains cannot do. Poetry is but one of the many channels through which the flow of philosophical ideas has sensibly swelled the world's store of sentiment and of knowledge. The standards of every age, individual, social, and political, have been modified to a greater or less extent by the influence of philosophical discussion. The doctrines of the schools become at last the maxims of the crowd. The eighteenth century philosophers cannot wash their hands of the blood of the French Revolution. Those essential principles of Protestantism which gave rise to civil as well as religious liberty, struck their roots deep in the soil of a religious philosophy. In Germany philosophical enlightenment gave stimulus to political life, and created a literature. Kant, Fichte, Schelling, and Hegel claim spiritual kinship with Herder, Goethe, Schiller, and Lessing. In England, we see that Gladstone, Morley, and Balfour have given serious thought to the problems of philosophy in the midst of pressing burdens of state, and the perplexities of public policy.

Philosophy, after all, is no dry-as-dust study. It is not a firing without aim and without projectile. Its problems are practical questions of the day. They are questions of every day, — of all time.

The true philosopher is a brave spirit; dauntless to discover, and bold to declare the truth at all hazard. He feels the inner constraint of his messages, and, as a prophet to his day and generation, he must needs speak, though the whole world cry to him, silence. With singleness of purpose he would cheerfully sacrifice place, friends, church, country, for the sake of truth. The philosopher's pursuits, moreover, have always stood as a tacit protest against the debasing influences of the materialistic tendencies of life, the greed of Mammon, and the deadening spell of utilitarian ideals; for amidst the levelling forces in the struggle for existence, the philosopher points to a higher ideal, and himself leads the way. He is a prophet as well as a schoolman. He has a mission to fulfil, as well as a theory to propound. He is under constraint to utter a message, as well as to acquire knowledge and to solve the perplexities of his own mind. The philosopher, nevertheless, is not always a poet or a prophet. He may be a man whose special calling seems to remove him very far from the sphere of philosophy, and may yet be a philosopher. A man's life, for example, may be devoted exclusively to the exacting demands of the legal profession, his thoughts absorbed in the weary round of law decisions and precedents, and theory may seemingly be of small concern to him, except so far as it may illumine practice; and yet he does not wholly ignore the philosophy of law. He must be conversant with the problems respecting the fundamental principles underlying equity and justice. The student of history pushes his research for facts with untiring perseverance, and yet the result of his labor is not a mere bundle of facts. It is such a grouping of consecutive events as shall reveal the whole, of which the separate facts are logically related parts. Thence it is but a step to a philosophy of history, and this step the historian is constrained to take. And so throughout the various spheres of life we find philosophical questions always emerging, — a philosophy of conduct, a philosophy of nature, a philosophy of art. Of life itself there must be a philosophy.

We therefore conclude that not to a special class, and that a restricted one, must the problems of philosophy be relegated. Those problems are a common heritage. He who ignores them despises his own birthright. To acquaint oneself with the questions which, in the various forms of statement, every generation from time immemorial has been forced to face, is not a privilege merely, it is a duty as well. If it is imperative that man should know the significant events of the world's history, it is equally imperative that he should be informed concerning the notable movements and epochs in the history of the world's thought, at any rate, so far as such history touches upon the verities of human existence and human welfare. A history of philosophy which records the achievements of man in the field of mind, discloses the same effort, the same struggle and conflict, hope and despair, victory and defeat, which characterize the more material and conspicuous deeds of history. The rise and fall of philosophies parallel the rise and fall of nations. The fortunes of philosophy have also their great motives, their heroes, their tragedies even. There is here, also, onward movement, the mighty sweep of a progressive development, whose end is the knowledge of the truth.

CHAPTER II

THE PROBLEMS OF PHILOSOPHY

WE have seen that philosophy is concerned with that which is, in contrast with that which seems to be. Its aim is to reveal the reality which underlies appearance. Its problem, therefore, is to discover the nature of reality, its various modes of manifestation, and their relations one to another. But what is reality? Is it not merely a term for the philosopher to conjure with, behind which he may craftily conceal his ignorance? For the philosopher may prate about truth, and reality, and the eternal verities, and what not. But do his words stand for clear intelligible ideas which the plain man can understand and appreciate? Let us examine more closely the significance of this vague word, reality. It may have several meanings, according to the different points of view which one takes. We may regard it as embodied in the physical world, the world of land and sea, of sky and trees, of sunshine and of storm. The real therefore will be to us that which we can touch and see, smell and taste, as one will say, "I know that is real for I can see it with my eyes." Seeing is believing, and the testimony of the senses is the superior court of appeal in controverted questions. But the world of reality may be regarded from quite a different point of view, as the world of consciousness, the mind of man, the experiences of the inner self, the Ego. Here is a world of phenomena interrelated and reciprocally dependent. It is a realm of ideas, of memory images, of fancy, of will, and of desire. The verities in this world cannot be seen, or measured, or weighed, and yet we do not hesitate to speak of them as realities; they are real as the love of friends is real, or the anger of a foe. The passion of a Romeo, the will of a Napoleon, the genius of a Goethe, the conception of a united fatherland in the fancy of a Bismarck, these are realities. A deeper significance of the real, and still further removed from the sphere of sense-perception is that of the reality which lies behind the world of sight and of sound, of thought and of desire, the real as eternal, "the hidden purpose of that Power which alone is great, and the myriad world His shadow." To some it may seem that we have here undertaken an excursion into the territory of the unreal; to others, however, such an idea appeals as the verity of verities.

The subject matter of philosophy, "that which is," that sphere of reality which seemed at first so obscurely outlined, we have found to comprise three definite divisions, nature, mind, and God. It is the province of philosophy not merely to consider reality under each one of these aspects separately, but also to consider the relations which obtain between them, that is, the relation between the world and man, between man and God, and between God and the world. Various lines of inquiry are thus suggested which serve to outline the separate spheres, and general scope of the various branches of philosophy, and to define the nature and manner of their reciprocal relations. Such a bird's-eye view of the territory of philosophy is called a philosophical encyclopædia.

That portion of the philosophical territory which we will first consider, is metaphysics. This is a term used originally by Aristotle to designate that part of his philosophy which came after (μέτα) his physics. It has come, however, to mean an inquiry which differs essentially from a physical mode of investigation. Physical research is connected with phenomena, their nature, description, and measurement, leading to the discovery and formulation of the laws of their behavior. Metaphysical investigation attempts to explain the fundamental nature of that which underlies phenomenal appearance, and constitutes its primary essence. Metaphysics goes behind the results of physics, seeking their deeper significance. There is, moreover, a second point of difference: metaphysics not only sees deeper, but with a more extended vision. For, while physics deals primarily with special problems such as electricity, magnetism, or heat, metaphysics, with a broad sweep of inquiry, puts the question as to the nature of being in general, and not any particular manifestation of it. Metaphysics is generally regarded as restricted in its scope to two special lines of inquiry: First, what is the nature of being in general? This is the problem of ontology. Second, what is the origin of the universe? This is the problem of cosmology.

In the problem of ontology we are confronted at once by an idea which is enveloped in the mists of indefiniteness. Being is so vague a term that it may mean anything or nothing. When a physical problem is presented for investigation, as, for example, the nature of electricity, the task before us is specific and definite; we know the problem that is set us even though we may despair of an adequate solution. But the question as to the nature of being presents evident difficulties; for how can we solve the problem when its very statement either conveys no meaning to our minds or so indefinite a one as to preclude any specific method of inquiry? However, the indefinite problem as to the nature of being has been narrowed, in metaphysical discussion, to quite a definite question: Are the phenomena of the universe through all possible phases of their manifestation, at the last analysis, of a material nature or of a spiritual, or are they of both a material and a spiritual nature? Is mind or matter at the basis of all things? The different theories advanced in answer to this question, the endless discussions and disputes, the philosophical schools which in consequence have arisen, all lie in the sphere of ontology, or the science of being.

In the proffered solutions of the problem of ontology, two tendencies may be indicated, one towards monism, the other towards dualism. Monism recognizes but one kind of being: It is either materialism, which reduces all psychical phenomena to a physical basis, that is, mind is regarded as a manifestation of matter, and thought, feeling, and will as merely brain products; or, we may have spiritualism, which explains everything material as the manifestation of a force which is psychical in its origin and nature, the world being regarded as a shadow world in which spirit embodies itself in outer forms which are merely the ghosts of reality. In one case mind is interpreted in terms of matter, and in the other, matter in terms of mind. Dualism, however, holds that there are two kinds of being, matter and mind, separate and distinct, yet capable of mutual interaction; and insists that there is a real world of mind and that there is a real world of matter.

The second distinctly metaphysical problem is that of cosmology, or the science of the world; not as to the nature of the world and its phenomena, for that would be the problem of ontology, but as to the origin of the world, quite irrespective of the question whether the world is all matter, or all mind, or partly matter and partly mind. The world may be explained mechanically, that is, any given phenomenon may be accounted for by referring it to its appropriate cause. Those who are satisfied with the explanation of the universe as an endless chain, or to use a more adequate simile, a network of intimately related causes and effects, are content to rest the case here. Concerning the supreme Being behind phenomena, they are either agnostics or atheists. The former say we know not whether there be a God; the latter say, we know there is no God.

In addition to the mechanical explanation of the universe, it is urged that there is a teleological explanation, that is, the discernment of an end (τέλος) or purpose in the midst of the mechanically related phenomena of existence. Thus the question of cosmology leads to the problem concerning the relation of God to the world. As to this relation there are various answers: polytheism, theism, deism, pantheism. Polytheism peoples the world with many gods, sometimes coöperating, sometimes in conflict, gods of one tribe warring with the god of a rival tribe. Deism, pantheism, and theism agree in affirming one only living and true God in opposition to polytheism. Deists believe in a God as creator of the universe, which, however, through the general laws and constitution of its elements, runs of itself without divine coöperation or intervention. Pantheism regards the universe as the comprehensive manifestation of God; God is everything, everything is God. Theism mediates between the tenets of deism, on the one hand, and those of pantheism, on the other, maintaining the proposition that God is distinct from the world, as opposed to pantheism, and yet operative in the world, as opposed to deism.

These two branches, ontology and cosmology, comprehend the problems of metaphysics. The term, metaphysics, however, is often used in a more general sense, as equivalent to all that transcends the physical methods of investigation and the mechanical point of view. The phrases, the metaphysics of ethics, the metaphysics of law, the metaphysics of art, indicate the wider use of the term.

The special province, however, of metaphysics is that which has been outlined above, as including ontology and cosmology.

Of the three aspects of reality, God, the world, and man, the study of man forms a separate branch of philosophy. And the term, man, as thus used, means mind, the ψύχη; hence the name, psychology, or the study of the psychical part of man's nature. In psychology we find certain general questions as to the origin, nature, or development of mind, or consciousness. These questions lie within the sphere of psychology considered as essentially a philosophical discipline. There are special problems, however, which require detailed investigation through observation and experiment. This is the field of experimental psychology, and constitutes a special science, closely related to and yet distinct from philosophical psychology. For instance, in the sphere of perception, philosophical questions emerge which relate to the theory of perception, the doctrine of its space and time conditions, to what extent the mind contributes to the process of perception, etc. Special psychology proceeds to investigate the phenomena of perception, to measure duration and intensity of the stimulus which produces the sensation. The tendency of modern research is to reduce psychology to a special experimental science, and to overlook the more general questions of a philosophical nature.

In the province of mind we find certain striking phenomena, a study of whose nature has given rise to much thought and to much discussion, and which has led to a special branch of philosophical inquiry, known as epistemology, or the theory of knowledge. It is a study of mind under its central aspect, that of the knowing mind. There are here two questions of special interest and significance which suggest themselves. The first is, what is the relation of the self which knows to the world which is known. We found that the question of ontology and cosmology referred to the nature and mutual relations of God and the world. The problems of philosophical psychology relate to the nature and origin of the conscious self. The question of epistemology concerns the relation of self in one of its principal functions, the self as knowing, to the world which the self comes to know. The answers to this question give rise to two opposed philosophical schools, that of realism and that of idealism. The former hold that the world is distinct from the self, which is aware of it, and exists independently of the observing consciousness. The idealist enters here a vigorous protest: "Not so fast. All that I know, really know, is at the last analysis the idea which is wholly within the sphere of consciousness. An object I know only so far as I apprehend the idea which constitutes my perception of it. The chair before my desk is present to my consciousness, vivid, clear, real; but I close my eyes, the chair vanishes. My consciousness of the chair is a mental fact, not a material thing. I know the mental fact, but what assurance have I that there is a material object corresponding to the mental image of it?" Has the object an existence independent of the perceiving mind? The idealist says emphatically, No! The realist urges his affirmative convictions quite as emphatically, and so the time-honored discussion runs on from one generation of philosophers to another.

There is still a second question as to the nature of knowledge, and this concerns its source. Does all our knowledge originate through experience, and especially through the avenues of the senses, or is there something in the very constitution of mind itself, which modifies the crude data of sense-perception, and thereby contributes in the construction of our world of knowledge? Is there anything which I may know to be true without putting it to the trial of my senses, or to the test of experiment, such as measuring, weighing, or counting? Do I know, for instance, prior to all experience, the truth of the proposition that the things which are equal to the same things are equal to each other, or must I prove it by actual experiment? Do I know, intuitively, that every event must have a cause, or does the conviction of this truth gradually dawn upon me with the widening spheres of observation and inference? Here, again, we have, in answer to such questions, two schools of philosophy, that of empiricism and that of rationalism. The empiricist insists that all knowledge is the outcome of experience, while the rationalist refers knowledge to the understanding as its primal source, whence arise necessary and universally valid principles of thought, which are prior to any experience, and which also condition and modify experience. The terms, *a priori* and *a posteriori*, are used to express this distinction, as regards knowledge which is before and knowledge which is after experience.

There is still another quarter of the philosophical territory, which comprises several distinct divisions which have as a common feature, that they inquire, not as to the nature of that which is, but of that which should be. Hence they are called normative; that is, they deal with a norm, or standard of being, which serves as an ideal according to which the phenomena in these several spheres are to be judged. There are three such disciplines: logic, which furnishes the norm of the true; ethics, the norm of the right or the good; and æsthetics, the norm of the beautiful. The first relates to the laws of reason; the second to an ideal of conduct; the third to the canons of taste. Logic, ethics, and æsthetics correspond roughly to the three main divisions of the mind, the intellect, the will, and the feelings.

The normative sciences differ from the others in that their judgments are judgments of valuation rather than of fact.

Psychology deals with the actual phenomena of consciousness, their origin, their nature, their causes and effects. Psychology is not concerned with the worth of a mental experience; right and wrong actions are accounted for indifferently upon a strict basis of mental interpretation. Ethics, however, discriminates between radically different kinds of actions, which have a certain worth as tested by some definite standard of conduct. In a like manner logic discriminates between the true and the false, and æsthetics between the beautiful, the harmonious, and symmetrical, on the one hand, and, on the other, the ugly, the discordant, and the unsymmetrical. The relation between the normative and the factual sciences, however, is most intimate. That which is followed as an ideal will be visionary and misleading unless grounded upon a comprehensive knowledge of the practical limitations and possibilities which the facts of mind necessitate. A study of the psychology of the reason must therefore precede the study of logic itself. The psychology of sensibility and of will must ground the theory of our moral consciousness. A fundamental knowledge of the emotions must precede an inquiry concerning the principles of æsthetics.

To resume, we have found that the ideas of the world, of man, and of God form the subject matter of the various philosophical sciences. The most general problem, that of being, in its most comprehensive significance without regarding its separate aspects of God, of man, and of the world, will lead us into the territory of ontology. The problem of the world and of the relation of the world to God, brings us into the neighboring province of cosmology. The problem of man, and by man is meant the mind in man, brings us into the field of philosophical psychology, and specializing in this territory as regards the relation of the knowing mind to the world, we reach the more restricted sphere of epistemology. Shifting our point of view to the guiding principles which operate as laws to our mental activities, and represent the ideal relations of the reasoning, willing, feeling man to the world, or to God, we find ourselves in the region of ethics, logic, and æsthetics. Such are the general features, roughly sketched, of the land which invites a more extended exploration.

CHAPTER III

THE PROBLEM OF BEING ("ONTOLOGY")

THE problem of being, or ontology, is that department of philosophy which treats, in its most comprehensive significance, the fundamental nature of that which is. What is the common essence of all substances midst their varying forms of manifestation? We may compare a plant, a stone, an animal, a man, and ask the question, Is there a common element at the basis of all these particular things from which the plant is fashioned after its kind, and the animal after its kind?

There is an unexpressed philosophy in the solemn words, "ashes to ashes, and dust to dust,"—a final reduction of all living forms to the inert mother of them all. But there is, on the other hand, a tendency to elevate matter into the sphere of mind, which is quite as pronounced as the attempt to reduce all things to matter. The problem of ontology, translated into popular phrase, is the much vexed question of the relations of mind and matter. The attempted solutions of this problem may be classified according to their expression of any one of the following characteristics : 1. Pluralism ; 2. Dualism ; 3. Monism.

Pluralism. — Pluralism is a theory of the universe which recognizes several fundamental elements of being, which may be regarded as analogous in their nature to the original elements of chemistry. They cannot be further reduced to simpler forms, nor derived from anything else, nor from each other. The earliest expression of this theory is found in the atomism of Democritus. He insisted that the world was made up of innumerable atoms, independent, self-existing bits of being, which could not be referred to a common source, and which gave no indication of possessing a common nature. Later in the history of philosophic thought we have another illustration of the pluralistic point of view in the so-called monads of Leibniz. These were refined atoms; centres of force rather than centres of matter and therefore at the last analysis of a psychical rather than a physical nature.

But even in these pluralistic explanations of being there is a tendency towards an indefinite sort of unity underlying the manifold differences. The teachings of Democritus imply a certain community of nature among his atoms, which were regarded as alike qualitatively though differing constitutionally in form and size, just as we say a rough block of marble and a statue are alike, yet different. Leibniz's doctrine manifested a like tendency, inasmuch as he regarded all his monads as possessing two fundamental characteristics in common, namely, the elements of perceiving and of striving. We find, therefore, that beneath the many of Democritus there was a materialistic substratum, indicating a oneness of origin, while beneath the many of Leibniz there was a psychical or soul basis as an abiding unity in the midst of the indefinite variety of monads.

Dualism. — If we imagine the tendencies in Democritus, and in Leibniz, as emerging at a common point, we will find the materialistic and spiritualistic conceptions uniting in that explanation of the nature of being which is known as dualism. This explanation conceives being in general, as partly material and partly spiritual in its manifestation. The expression of dualism is represented by the doctrines of Descartes, who is regarded as the father of modern philosophy. According to him the essence of matter is extension, that is, the occupying of some portion of space, the spread-outedness of a body. The essence of mind, however, is thought. These two essences are radically distinct, the one, *res extensa*, extended being, the other, *res cogitans*, or thinking being. The theory of dualism further holds that the relation of extended matter to the thinking mind is one of mutual interaction. It is known as the "reaction" theory; at the presence of one form of being, as stimulus operating according to its proper mode of activity, the corresponding form of being reacts in response according to its own mode of manifestation. There are many difficulties, however, which are connected with this theory. All sensory stimulus is essentially motion, as is seen in the waves of sound vibrations which strike the ear, or the light waves impinging upon the retina. How, then, can that which is essentially motion influence or act upon that whose essence is thought? There is no common denominator here.

No theory of cause and effect, as we understand cause, can explain the relation between such disparate phenomena. There have been, however, several attempts to explain this difficulty, as Leibniz's celebrated doctrine of preëstablished harmony. Leibniz maintained that body and mind only seem to interact, but that there is no real connection between the two. The mind wills and an arm moves simultaneously, but the will does not move the arm. The thought-sphere is a closed circle; so, also, the motor-sphere. They act, however, in unison according to a prearranged programme, — a preëstablished harmony which a divine mind alone could conceive, establish, and execute. Another device to reconcile the difficulties in the case is that known as occasionalism, a theory associated with the name of Geulincx, the most brilliant representative of the Cartesian school. He held that God intervenes upon the occasion of every volition in order to stimulate the motor activity which the mind by itself is incapable of originating, and in like manner upon the occasion of every physical stimulus, there is a similar intervention to produce a corresponding mental activity resulting in sensation and perception.

Both of these views negative the freedom of man. The power of human initiative is lost. Man becomes virtually an automaton in the loss of his individuality and responsibility. He is the harp of a thousand strings played upon by a divine hand, but not a man!

Monism. — This is the theory of being which recognizes but one sort of essence in everything, however manifold may seem the variety of nature's manifestations. There are three distinct forms of monism: —

(*a*) Materialism, which regards mind as a form or product of matter.

(*b*) Spiritualism, which regards matter as a form or product of mind.

(*c*) The Identity theory, which regards matter and mind as different phases in the manifestation of one and the same being, which is itself neither matter nor mind.

Materialism. — Materialism would reduce all mental phenomena to simple effects or by-products of matter. This theory fortifies itself by the evident fact that there is no perception, no memory, no will, no emotion, without a corresponding modification of the brain tissue. The philosophical postulate of materialism is expressed in the epigrammatical proposition, "No psychosis without neurosis," *i.e.* it is impossible to have mind function without brain function, no thought without an indispensable accompanying change in the cerebral centres. If you injure the brain, consciousness ceases wholly, or in part; or, at least, the normal functions are seriously deranged. Stimulants excite, anæsthetics benumb the sensibilities. In the light of these indisputable facts many are led to the conviction which is expressed in the words of the eminent French physician, Cabanis: "Thought is a function of the brain as digestion is a function of the stomach, and the secretion of bile the function of the liver." The tenets of materialism are nowhere more sententiously epitomized than in the gross pun of Feuerbach, one of the most pronounced of the German materialists: "Der Mensch ist was er isst," Man is (ist) what he eats (isst).

The materialist claims that he holds an impregnable position in entrenching himself behind the accepted doctrine of the conservation of energy, which precludes the possibility of there being any force in the universe which cannot be expressed in mechanical terms. For, as heat generates steam, and steam produces motion, and motion initiates an electric current which appears as transformed energy in the arc light or motor appliances, and yet through all these different manifestations there is only a transfer of energy from one form to another, no new energy being added, and none lost, so, also, the energy produced by vibratory sound waves is transformed by impact upon the tympanum of the ear into a nerve disturbance, which, in turn, is transmitted by the sensory nerve channels to the brain, there producing an effect after its kind. The idea of a manifestation other than material appearing at the end of a series of causally related phenomena, which, at the beginning and through all the intermediate stages, is essentially mechanical, does violence, the materialist would insist, to the fundamental and universal laws of matter as expressed in the doctrine of the conservation of energy. The materialists, therefore, in their line of defence maintain these two closely allied positions, the unbroken continuity of the physiological nerve-brain circuit. and the law of the conservation of energy; they insist that not only is there then no place, but also no necessity for any additional force which differs in kind from matter.

There is still another doctrine, known as the parsimony of causes, to which the materialists appeal. The doctrine is, that when a known cause will adequately account for any given effect, it is a work of supererogation to search for additional causes to explain the effect in question. Physical causes are all sufficient; why then waste time and thought in a fruitless quest beyond the sphere of the known and the material?

We come now to consider some of the difficulties of the materialistic position which naturally suggest themselves. In the first place, their argument, based upon the doctrine of the conservation of energy, may be turned against themselves. It is in this respect a veritable two-edged sword, for inasmuch as at the beginning of the series and through all its sequences we have an unbroken line of mechanical causation, and yet the fact remains that the final term is manifestly of such a nature that between it and the other terms of the series there is no likeness, and no common factor, the conclusion seems necessitated that this final term cannot be referred to a mechanical antecedent as its sole cause. It must be other than material, namely, that which we call psychical. With the same premises there are thus two conflicting inferences. Given a mechanical series ending in a psychical phenomenon, the materialist draws the inference, that the psychical phenomenon is not really such but only seems to be; that it is in reality purely physical, for the matrix from which it emerges is physical. The opposed view insists that the final term is so radically different in kind as to enjoin the materialist from attempting to correlate the material and mental phenomena under one and the same law of universal causation. This latter view acknowledges that the mental and material are invariably found together, and yet contends that it is a gratuitous assumption to insist that they are connected as cause and effect.

In any effect, moreover, there is always evidence of the energy which was present in the cause and was operative in producing that effect. That energy may be, it is true, transformed to a great extent, but the form, however changed, will always readily show traces of a material origin, inasmuch as it will evidence itself in some one or other of the various manifestations of motion. In the phenomena of consciousness, however, in our thoughts, desires, volitions, we have no trace of a material origin. That which is thought or feeling cannot be translated into terms of matter and motion. Moreover, if the material energy has been transformed into psychical force, there is an evident loss of material energy as such. This, however, would contravene the doctrine of the conservation of energy which requires a constant amount of energy which cannot possibly sustain a loss, however insignificant that loss may seem to be. The conception of an endless series of cause and effect in which all phenomena of the universe, without exception, are to be found, is a convenient and most comfortable theory. It simplifies the problems of existence, and dismisses many perplexing questions. The phenomena of experience, however, as they appear in consciousness are too complex, too unique, to be forced into the closed circle of physical phenomena. The explanation of mind, as the product of material forces, is, moreover, necessarily stated in terms and by means of concepts essentially mental. We are confronted, therefore, with this anomaly, that the mind is accounted for by an idea, namely, the idea of universal causation, which idea must have been itself constructed by the mind which it purports to explain. There is here evidently a "weak arguing and a fallacious drift."

The doctrine of materialism runs counter to the theory of evolution, although the materialists very confidently refer to this theory as fortifying their own position. If consciousness is a by-product of cerebral functions, and is in no sense a real factor amid the causal series of physiological excitations and corresponding reactions, then the phenomena of consciousness can have been of no real advantage to the organism in the process of its development. For, if it is not a real factor and does not initiate any activity or modify, in any degree whatever, its physical accompaniments, then it cannot influence the development of the organism one way or the other. But it is one of the essentials of evolution that whatever function fails to influence the growth of the organism tends therefore to disappear entirely in the process of development. In passing, however, from a lower to a higher order of animal life we are struck with the growing complexity and scope of the phenomena of consciousness. They do not tend to disappear. On the contrary, we are confronted with the palpable fact that consciousness with its power of initiative has proved the potent factor in the activities and achievements of man, which has assured the preservation of the species and its dominance over the entire realm of nature. Consciousness is therefore a principal factor and not a secondary product in the evolution of man.

Materialism is an insidious doctrine, appealing especially to many in this age, because it seems to be confirmed by the results of science and to be in strict accord with the scientific spirit and point of view. For this reason Lange, in his *History of Materialism*, speaks of Democritus as the one among all the ancient philosophers who was most truly modern, because his essentially materialistic conceptions were most akin to the present day mode of regarding the universe of physical phenomena. The brilliant coterie of eighteenth century philosophers in France, among whom La Mettrie, Diderot, D'Holbach, Helvétius, and Cabanis shone conspicuously, clothed their teachings in the garb of such fascinating plausibility that to a superficial mind they seem to be demonstratively conclusive. In the nineteenth century, materialism is more distinctively German than French; the chief apostles of

German materialism are Feuerbach, Moleschott, Büchner, Vogt, and Haeckel. They reinforced the earlier position by an appeal to the enormous mass of scientific facts which the marvellous researches of the nineteenth century have revealed. The influence of such teaching has been far-reaching and pervasive.

Professor Flint, in his *Anti-Theistic Theories*, has spoken very significantly of this influence: "But it is not to be hoped that materialism will ever quite be got rid of, so long as the constitution of the human mind and the character of human society remain substantially what they are. Physical nature and its laws explain much, and so long as the human mind is prone to exaggeration, and education is imperfect and one-sided, and society is more under the influence of the seen than the unseen, of the temporal than the eternal, it may be anticipated that many will fancy that matter and motion explain everything, and this fancy is the essence of materialism. Thus, materialism is a danger to which individuals and societies will always be more or less exposed. The present generation, however, which is growing up, will obviously be very specially exposed to it; as much so, perhaps, as any generation in the history of the world. Within the last thirty years the great wave of spiritualistic or idealistic thought, which has borne to us on its bosom most of what is of chief value in the nineteenth century, has been receding and decreasing; and another, which is in the main driven by materialistic forces, has been gradually rising behind it, vast and threatening. It is but its crests that we at present see; it is but a certain vague shaking produced by it that we at present feel; but we shall probably soon enough fail not both to see and feel it fully and distinctly."[1]

Spiritualism. — The view of the universe which reduces all phenomena to a manifestation of some kind of psychical force is spiritualism. Leibniz may be regarded as the father of this theory in its

---

[1] Flint, *Anti-Theistic Theories*, pp. 98, 99.

modern form at least. In ancient times Plato was as essentially spiritualistic in his teachings as Democritus was materialistic. Leibniz's monads were regarded as centres of force which, in all cases, could be traced to a common source, essentially psychical in its nature. Schopenhauer defined this psychic force underlying material phenomena as essentially will whose striving initiates motion. As spiritualism is a view diametrically opposed to materialism, it might seem at first glance that the arguments which are valid against materialism would make for the support of spiritualism. Yet materialism false does not argue spiritualism true; for the most cogent arguments against materialism bear upon its monistic features, and these arguments also make against spiritualism regarded as a monistic philosophy. The transition from mind to matter is as bewilderingly mysterious as the transition from matter to mind. The two disparate phenomena cannot be brought under the single category either of matter or of mind. Spiritualism, however, as a monistic system has a more rational ground for claiming to be an exclusive philosophy than materialism, for the elements of consciousness, the psychical part of man's nature, are more adequately expressive of the Ego, the real self, than the material. The world with its phenomena of cause and effect, the endless series of mechanical sequences, and of chemical reactions, the manifold processes of vital growth, seem foreign to the inner world of self, which is essentially a world of consciousness. We know nothing of matter pure and simple, only of matter as it is perceived and translated into the terms of conscious experience. The spiritualist, therefore, insists that it is easier to explain matter by mind than to explain mind by matter, inasmuch as the mental is the more familiar of the two, being, as it is, the mode in which the self finds its essential expression.

The hypothesis, however, which conceives all phenomena as the manifestation of a psychical energy presupposes rather gratuitously, it must be confessed, a knowledge of the fundamental constitution of matter which the possibilities of exact observation do not warrant. Every atom in the universe may be only a centre of psychical force, and yet, as we cannot demonstrate this, we should not attempt to construct a theory upon it.

The Theory of Identity. — This theory regards mind and matter as different phases of one and the same being, which is neither mind nor matter. The physical and the psychical phenomena are regarded as two closed circuits, each complete in itself; the movements, however, within the one sphere run parallel to the activities of the other. The theory is often called the theory of parallelism. Physical energy is wholly accounted for in the physiological effects upon the nervous system; no vestige of it is available to account for the psychical manifestations. The latter, therefore, must be referred to a sphere of activity of their own kind, in which they operate in such a manner that the phenomena of the two spheres manifest themselves synchronously and harmoniously. The parallelism of the two spheres may be illustrated by the correspondence which exists between a connected series of sounds on the one hand, and the interpretation of these sounds in a series of connected thoughts. The sound is physical merely, but the mind recognizes a thought value corresponding to each varying shade of sound. When, however, a foreigner hears a language unknown to him, there is no such mental correspondence, the inner circuit is not paralleled to the outer. The sounds are unintelligible and remain sounds, mere sounds. But even a bare sound without significance has a corresponding psychical value, for the sensation of the sound differs from the stimulus, which is the antecedent of the sensation. This parallelism obtains throughout our whole conscious experience from the lower level of correspondence between stimulus and sensation, to the higher plain of correspondence between outer symbols and the inner thought processes which interpret these symbols.

It is urged, moreover, that there is a proportionality as well as parallelism between the two spheres, so that the ratio between the amount of stimulus and the corresponding intensity of the sensation can be definitely measured, and that the resulting law which formulates such a relation is capable of precise expression. As thus stated, parallelism has become a working hypothesis which underlies all investigations in experimental psychology, and is accepted as such by monists and dualists alike. There is, however, an additional assumption which some would regard as a necessary consequence of the foregoing, and which, in attempting to discover the ground of the parallelism in addition to the statement of it as a fact, transforms the working hypothesis into a metaphysical explanation. It is contended that the parallelism of the physical phenomena of the one sphere and the activities of consciousness in the other implies a substantial identity underlying this twofold manifestation. Matter and mind, therefore, must be regarded as complementary phases of one and the same ground substance which is neither matter nor mind. This is the view of Spinoza in earlier times, more recently of Herbert Spencer, and, in the circle of experimental psychologists, the view substantially of Fechner. This theory is often called Neo-Spinozism. The popularity of this view is indicated, in a measure, by the present revival of interest in the writings of Spinoza.

It is to be noticed that there is a tendency to emphasize either the material or the mental in one's conception of the nature of the underlying substance in which the two are supposed to inhere. Thus Leibniz, in following Spinoza, placed the emphasis upon the psychical phase to such an extent as to make it the sole essence of all being. On the other hand, the English philosopher, Hobbes, regarded the material rather than the psychical as the more fundamental and essential of the two. In this Hobbes expresses the conviction of many of the modern scientific investigators in the field of experimental psychology. The doctrine of parallelism has this to its credit, that it has brought the psychical activities to the fore as something not wholly explained, at least as by-products of the material.

A criticism of the theory will reveal several weak points in its structure. In the first place it assumes an accompanying psychical manifestation for every physical phenomenon, whereas we are only aware of this parallelism in connection with a limited portion of the material universe, namely, the sphere of brain modifications. Mr. Romanes, in his admirable essay, *The World as Eject*, indicates the possibility of there being a world consciousness in connection with all forms of matter, similar to the consciousness which is manifest in connection with brain activities. He speaks of the world as eject, using that term to suggest the possible function of consciousness associated with the world, which may correspond to that form of consciousness which we have always associated exclusively with the

Ego, or the subject. A similar idea we find in the lines of Browning:—

" For many a thrill
Of kinship I confess to, with the powers
Called Nature; animate, inanimate,
In parts or in the whole, there's something there
Man-like that somehow meets the man in me."

There may be a soul of the world, there may be, as has already been said, a psychical side, of which we are not aware, to every atom in the universe, and the psychical side, like the moon, may show us ever but the one face, the other forever in the shadow; but, at best, this is only a conjecture, it presents no solid foundation upon which to rest a theory.

Moreover, we know from psychological investigation that the physiological circuit must reach a certain degree of intensity as regards any stimulus, before there is a corresponding sensation. We do not always hear the persistent summons of the alarm clock. The degree of intensity which the stimulus must reach in order to produce consciousness of a sensation, is not a constant quantity. It differs with individuals; it differs in the experience of a single person at different times, and under different circumstances, depending largely upon his attention at the moment, or upon his passing interests. The Indian guide perceives a whole world of sights and sounds to which his companion is blind; or, if that same Indian is hot on the trail of a foe, he, too, may find his field of perception restricted by the fever of warfare. We find, again, that there is a complete cessation of consciousness in sleep; stimulation of the end-organs of sense is followed by no parallel manifestation in consciousness. In an extreme manner, this is seen in cases of brain injury, where consciousness in certain modes of its manifestation ceases altogether, yet upon restoration of the injured part, the chain of ideas is resumed precisely at the point where it was broken off. The physiological circuit is active throughout the interval of sleep or brain injury. What psychical activity has been going on parallel to it, and yet of which there is no consciousness whatsoever?

These considerations indicate certain gaps in the continuity of parallelism, and prove the extreme difficulty of coördinating perfectly the two systems of material and conscious activities.

There is, moreover, a vagueness which envelops that indefinite something which is neither matter nor mind, yet lies at the basis of either system, synthesizing the two.

However the point of view may be shifted, the manifest disparity between motion and thought, between matter and mind, still confronts us. It was the despair of reaching any satisfactory solution of this perplexing problem which led Du Bois-Reymond to utter his famous comment concerning it: "Ignoramus! Ignorabimus!"

CHAPTER IV

THE WORLD PROBLEM ("COSMOLOGY")

THE world problem, or cosmology, proved of special interest to the ancient Greek mind. The earliest philosophical inquiries were concerned with the possibility of discovering some primal element in the world structure to which the various conflicting and interacting phenomena might be reduced. The speculations which mark the beginnings of Greek philosophy were crude and fanciful, and yet the spirit of these early thinkers was commendable, for they were searchers after a unity underlying the world phenomena, and as such they are worthy the name of philosophers. Of these thinkers, one of the earliest was Thales, who lived about 600 B.C. He regarded water as the universal substratum, of which all things were more or less complex manifestations. To Anaximander, however, the universal atmosphere seemed to be the true mother of all existing things; and, in a similar manner, Anaximenes regarded air, or breath, as the source of all being. Heraclitus saw in fire the essence of all things. He regarded fire as the cause of a universal motion, everything being derived from it and everything striving to return to the source whence it emanated. The universe presented to him a scene of constant change, of perpetual flow; there was no stability and no abiding unity. Still another old Greek, Empedocles, had his peculiar view of the elemental source, which he declared to be of a fourfold nature, — earth, air, fire, and water.

In the midst of these puerile conjectures there were, however, certain intimations of a more philosophical explanation. There was a tendency, early manifesting itself, to discern beneath all phenomena a substantial unity, and, moreover, to regard this unifying principle as something other than material. Thus Xenophanes speaks of the source of all things as a Being which is one and infinite; and Parmenides speaks of the same as the All-One. Also, in addition to the four material elements of Empedocles, — earth, air, fire, and water, — that philosopher insists upon a spiritual principle, love, as the actuating force behind the material elements, which are to be regarded merely as its agents.

According to Anaxagoras, there is in the universe an organizing and unifying power, which he calls the νοῦς, *i.e.* the mind, or reason, and this principle renders the world a cosmos instead of a chaos; to its purposeful activity are due the order, harmony, and beauty of the universe.

Thus it may be seen that while the question of the underlying world structure was originally answered in material terms, yet a stage was soon reached in the unfolding and deepening thought of the old world where only a spiritualistic answer was deemed satisfactory. The problems of cosmology resulting in a solution which maintained a spiritual principle at the basis of the world fabric, naturally led to deeper questions as to the more precise nature of such a spiritual principle. Thus the world problem became at its last analysis an inquiry concerning the being and nature of God. Is there an underlying unity amidst the manifold world phenomena? and is this unity a spiritual principle, which manifests itself in a supreme Being, whom we may regard as the Author and Governor of the universe?

The answers to these questions vary from an absolute denial of the being of God, on the one hand to an absolute identification of all existence with the being of God, on the other. The early negative position was formulated in the atomism of Democritus. According to his teaching, as we have seen, the world was composed of an indefinite number of indestructible particles acting independently through forces within themselves toward necessarily determined ends. All phenomena were thus reduced to the "mechanics of atoms." There was no such thing as purpose or design, only an inevitable fate swaying the affairs of men. In such a system, there is no need, and in fact no place for the being of God. Democritus was the natural father of materialism with its atheistical implications. The atomism of Democritus was developed at length in the system of Lucretius as expressed in his didactic poem, *De natura rerum*. We find it also in the teachings of Epicurus and of the Epicurean school. The mechanical explanation of the universe, however, was not satisfactory to the Greek mind, and therefore from that early day to the present there have always been many who have sought a more philosophical solution of the problem. The inadequacy of the mechanical view of the universe is aptly stated by Windelband: —

"An archæologist of nature may trace back the genealogy of life, the origination of one species from another, according to mechanical principles as far as possible; he will always be obliged to stop with an *original organization*, which he cannot explain through the mere mechanism of inorganic matter."[1]

---

[1] Windelband, *History of Philosophy*, p. 565.

Among those, however, who are not satisfied with the mechanical explanation of the universe, there is a considerable diversity of opinion concerning the being and nature of that spiritualistic principle which, it is affirmed, must lie at the basis of all the world phenomena. The resulting theories are known under the names of polytheism, theism, deism, and pantheism. They form the several positive answers to the great world problem. We will consider them separately.

Polytheism. — This was the early superstitious belief in gods many and lords many. As a philosophy it has no valid claim for serious consideration, and may be relegated to the sphere of mythological speculation. The dawning philosophical sense of the Greeks could not abide the crude anthropomorphism of the polytheistic belief, that is, the representation of the gods in the form of men with like passions and limitations. There was an early recognition of the fact that God must be one and spiritual, rather than many and of human habits and propensities. A most earnest protest against these human gods was raised by Xenophanes, one of the earliest of the Greek philosophers. Aristotle's description of him is very striking: "Casting his eyes upwards at the immensity of heaven he declared that *The One* is God." Xenophanes thus became the father of a monotheistic philosophy, which regards God as one and spiritual.

Monotheism. — This theory, whose very name sharply contrasts it with polytheism, is a belief in the one supreme Being, the power behind the world and its phenomena and the unifying principle in nature and in human life. Monotheism in its distinction from polytheism embraces the several systems of theism, deism, and pantheism.

Of these, deism is the belief which regards the Deity as existing outside the world which He once created, sustaining to it a relation similar to that which the artisan sustains to the work which his hands and brain have fashioned. Deism, therefore, emphasizes that attribute of God, which is designated as His transcendence, that is, the idea of God as dwelling apart from the universe of men and things. Pantheism is a natural reaction from deism; as the latter emphasizes the transcendence of God to the exclusion of His immanence, so the former emphasizes His immanence to the exclusion of His transcendence. God's immanence is the manifestation of Himself in His works; if, therefore, God manifests Himself completely in His works, and His transcendence is denied or ignored, then it follows that God is everything, and everything is God. Theism holds a mean between these two extremes.

Theism. — This attempts to harmonize in one consistent theory the two seemingly conflicting ideas of God's transcendence and of God's immanence. It is differentiated from deism in that it insists upon the sustaining and operating presence of God in all phenomena of the universe. Theism denies the possibility of an "absentee God." It differs, however, on the other hand, from pantheism in affirming the existence of a real distinction between God and His works, between the Creator and the creature, especially as this distinction is emphasized in the consciousness of a self which refuses to be absorbed in the great All of pantheism. Thus theism is an attempt to synthesize within a higher unity the two opposed ideas of transcendence and immanence, and which regards God as manifesting Himself in and through His works, and yet as a personality, distinct from them.

Deism. — Deism has a greater affinity with polytheism than either pantheism or theism. It is a refined form of polytheism. It is true that it disavows gods many, but its one god is conceived after the similitude of human beings according to the manner of the polytheistic conception. The God of the deist is an "enlarged man," an artificer rather than a creator; the world is regarded as a stupendous mechanism rather than a manifestation of the life of the supreme Being. Deism flourished in the eighteenth century. Its founder was Lord Herbert of

Cherbury. Among its most eminent representatives we find Locke and Voltaire. It developed within the sphere of its adherents two opposed tendencies, one leading towards pantheism, the other towards atheism. They were natural reactions from the artificial doctrines of deism. The violent separation of God and nature might leave the impression, on the one hand, that nature needs no God to explain her manifestations and phenomena, or, on the other hand, the felt need of God in and through nature's manifold being might become so emphasized as to result in pantheism, — the swing of the pendulum to the extreme opposite of deism.

Pantheism. — The universe is regarded as the manifestation of God, solely and completely. God is all. A striking statement of pantheistic belief, at the same time a criticism of deism, we find in the words of Goethe: "What were a God who only gave the world a push from without, or let it spin around His finger? I look for a God who moves the world from within, who fosters nature in Himself, Himself in nature; so that naught of all that lives and moves and has its being in Him ever forgets His force or His spirit."[1]

Dr. Martineau has said that pantheism marks a temperament rather than a system, the immediate vision of the poet rather than the reflective interpretation of the philosopher.[2] The atmosphere of mysticism which envelops pantheistic speculation is naturally most alluring to the poet, and especially the poet to whom nature has revealed the spirit of its being. One of the most profound and subtle expressions of pantheistic interpretation we find in the "Lines Composed above Tintern Abbey," where Wordsworth speaks in the following vein of nature's spell over his soul: —

---

[1] Was wär' ein Gott, der nur von aussen stiesse
Im Kreis das All am Finger laufen liesse!
Ihm ziemt's, die Welt im Innern zu bewegen,
Natur in Sich, Sich in Natur zu hegen
So dass, was in Ihm lebt und webt und ist,
Nie Seine Kraft, nie Seinen Geist vermisst.

[2] Martineau, *A Study of Religion*, Vol. II, p. 141.

"For I have learned
To look on nature, not as in the hour
Of thoughtless youth; but hearing oftentimes
The still, sad music of humanity,
Nor harsh nor grating, though of ample power
To chasten and subdue. And I have felt
A presence that disturbs me with the joy
Of elevated thoughts: a sense sublime
Of something far more deeply interfused,
Whose dwelling is the light of setting suns,
And the round ocean, and the living air,
And the blue sky, and in the mind of man:
A motion and a spirit that impels
All thinking things, all objects of all thought,
And rolls through all things."

Pantheism takes two forms, which do not differ, however, fundamentally. The one identifies God completely with the world of being, coming to His highest manifestation in the consciousness of man. From the lowest to the highest, from the simplest to the most complex forms of this manifestation, all is God. The other view emphasizes the divine as the only reality and reduces the facts of existence to a mere appearance, the shadowy semblance of reality. While the former view denies all difference between God and the world, including man, the latter insists that the seeming difference must be regarded as a mental illusion, having no basis in reality. In either case, God's immanence is magnified to the exclusion of His transcendence. It is a convenient philosophy, the reference of everything to God; it unties many hard knots, it cuts in twain many more. It was a veritable stroke of genius that suggested the reduction of the manifold variety of the universe to one simple category. We feel instinctively the seriousness and the profundity of thought which characterizes the creed of pantheism. This is felt in a peculiar manner in Hegel's admirable statement of the pantheistic belief: —

"The ancient philosophers have described God under the image of a round ball. But if that be His nature, God has unfolded it; and in the actual world He has opened the closed shell of truth into a system of Nature, into a State-system, a system of Law and Morality, into the system of the world's History. The shut fist has become an open hand, the fingers of which reach out to lay hold of man's mind, and draw it to Himself. Nor is the human mind a self-involved intelligence, blindly moving within its own secret recesses. It is no mere feeling and groping about in a vacuum, but an intelligent system of rational organization. Of that system, Thought is the summit in point of form, and Thought may be described as the capability of going beyond the mere surface of God's self-expansion, — or rather as the capability, by means of reflection upon it, of entering into it, and then, when the entrance has been secured, of retracing in thought God's expansion of Himself. To take this trouble is the express duty and end of ends set before the thinking mind, ever since God laid aside His rolled-up form and revealed Himself."[1]

That which characterizes the point of view of pantheism, and at the same time marks the point of departure from deistic conceptions, is the pantheistic interpretation of the teleological argument for the being of God. The teleological argument is based upon the evidence of design which

[1] Wallace, *The Logic of Hegel*, p. 26.

is manifested throughout the varied adaptations of means to ends in nature. The teleological ideas of the deists may be most adequately represented by an analogy which they insist exists between the product of a mechanic's labor, such as a watch, and the world which is similarly conceived as the handiwork of God. As the watch contains within its own mechanism evidence of a designer and maker, so the orderly adjustments and purposeful contrivances in nature indicate a great and wise Designer.

The pantheist, however, repudiates this conception of teleology as being external and mechanical. In its stead, he would substitute an immanent teleology, that is, a force within the organism moulding it into its proper form and adapting its organs to their appropriate functions, and all parts to harmonious ends. Instead of the conception of an architect planning and fashioning an organism from without, there is the conception of an architectonic principle operative within the organism, fulfilling its own ends. This immanent finality reaches its most perfect development and highest realization in the purposive activities of man. It is the power within nature and man which to the pantheist evidences the Divine Being. The great Designer, therefore, could not have worked *upon* the world materials, and have fashioned them into form and life from without, for only *in* and *through* them does He manifest Himself.

At this point, theism is in perfect accord with pantheism. The immanence of God and the doctrine of immanent finality appeal to the theist as well. The theist takes exception, not to that which pantheism asserts, but to that which pantheism denies, or ignores, namely, the transcendence of God. To equate God with the universe without remainder, exhausts His being and manifestly limits Him to a definite comprehension within finite bounds. He is no longer the Eternal, the Infinite One! God is in nature, and yet He is more than nature. Spinoza, the pantheist who was styled the God-intoxicated man, was led to acknowledge a real distinction, first insisted upon in Arabian philosophy, between *Natura naturans* and *Natura naturata*, that is, nature as Creator and nature as creature. In this distinction lies the essence of the theistic contention. Moreover, the absorption of all things in God reduces man's personality to zero. This meets with a very determined protest from our self-asserting consciousness, which refuses to be merged in the universal All. In the relations between God and man, as in the relations between God and the world, it is still possible to hold that God manifests Himself to man in the still small voice within, and yet that man himself is more than a manifestation of God. There is a revelation of God to man in the light of reason, in the voice of conscience, and in the inspiration of the truth, yet it is a revelation *to* man; the self receives, the self is moved, the self is preserved in its integrity as the self, the man, and not as God. Dr. Martineau enters a most earnest plea for the due recognition of a distinct selfhood: "What then becomes of the human personality when all its characteristics are thus conveyed over to the Supreme Mind? The very terms in which it is described abolish it. If truth, if righteousness, if love and faith, are all an influx of foreign light, the endowments, in virtue of which we are susceptible of them, are mere passive and recipient organs on to which they are delivered, and we have no agency of our own. But a *reason* that does no thinking for itself, a *conscience* that flings aside no temptation and springs to no duty, *affection* that toils in no chosen service of love, a *religious sentiment* that waits for such faith as may come into it, simply negative their own functions and disappear."[1]

There is a tendency, strange to say, in the development of pantheistic thought towards materialism. It is characteristic of any extreme position that it provokes a reactionary movement in the direction of its opposite. Pantheism, in identifying God with the world, leads some of its

[1] Martineau, *A Study of Religion*, Vol. II, p. 180.

adherents to ask the question: "If the world is everything, why call it God? The only story the world tells us of itself, is the story of material atoms and mechanical relations. Is not the idea of God, therefore, wholly illusory?"

Such questioning has appealed to many who were originally avowed pantheists. Several of the Hegelian pantheists developed along these lines. They are spoken of as "Hegelians of the Left." The change of front is notably illustrated in the dissolving views of Feuerbach, who, in his *Thoughts on Death and Immortality*, regards the disappearance of man's personality in the divine All as the true immortality, and yet, nevertheless, became later one of the most pronounced advocates of a gross materialism.

Materialism is the bringing of God down to the level of nature, and pantheism is bringing nature up to God. It is easy to see, therefore, how a common point of view may prove to be a point of departure whence diverge lines of opposed thought.

CHAPTER V

THE PROBLEM OF MIND ("PSYCHOLOGY")

THE study of the mind suggests certain philosophical questions of a general nature, as well as the special problems of a strict psychology. The distinction between the philosophy of mind, and the mind considered as the subject matter of a special science, is a distinction as old as Aristotle, and yet one which, in the history of philosophy, has often been overlooked or ignored. The modern point of view regards psychology exclusively as a special science. The philosophical aspect of psychology is flatly questioned. There are, however, certain philosophical questions which thrust themselves upon one's consideration, although it may be maintained that there are no satisfactory answers to them.

Of these questions there are two of chief importance.

1. As to the being and nature of the soul, the ψύχη of man.

2. As to the primary mode of psychical activity, whether it is of the nature of intellection or volition.

The Substantialists and Actualists. — The problem as to the being and nature of a soul starts the inquiry, whether there is a separate self distinct from the phenomena of consciousness, or whether the term, soul, is merely an expression denoting the sum total of conscious activities. The former is the view of the so-called substantialists, of whom Descartes is an eminent representative. They regard the soul as a real substance, a unifying principle, of which the several mental modes and activities are separate manifestations.

On the other hand, the view of the opposed school, the actualists, is that all that we know are merely the states of consciousness, *actual* happenings, related to each other, it is true, and mutually modifying each other, but in no way unified in the sense of being all manifestations of an underlying substance in which they all inhere.

According to this idea, consciousness is represented as a stream of passing events, with no enduring and abiding ground. This view we find expressed in the ancient teachings of Indian philosophy. Gautama, the Buddha, insisted that belief in Attavāda, the doctrine of the separate individuality of the self, was one of the chief heresies by which man is insidiously led into error. He compared the human individual to a chariot, which was only a chariot so long as it was a complete whole, of seat, axle, wheels, pole, etc., — beneath the sum of the parts there was no substratum which was the real chariot, — so there can be no substance underlying the ever changing experiences of consciousness. There being no separate self, the idea of a soul and an immortal existence apart from an absorption in the Eternal Being was a delusion of the mind and a snare of the heart. Such was the doctrine of Buddha, and it has its modern counterpart.

From the standpoint of the substantialist it is urged that as the material phenomena of the world are referred, each to some appropriate material substance of which it is the manifestation, so, also, in reference to the consciousness the various phenomena must inhere in some analogous mental substratum, which we call mind, or the soul, or the self. As we say that odor, color, form are attributes of one and the same substance, as a flower, so also the will, desire, emotion are functions of one and the same mental substance, the underlying self. From the necessities of the case there can be no *proof* of the existence of the self, for the self cannot demonstrate its own existence except in a direct awareness of a continued identity and prevailing unity in the midst of the varying experiences of time and space. As Kant says, the idea of the soul as an unconditioned real unity of all the phenomena of the inner sense is indeed as little capable of proof as it is of refutation. It must be regarded simply as evidencing itself in an immediate deliverance of consciousness. This direct testimony of consciousness is held, on the part of the actualists, to be wholly illusory. It is urged that there are certain purely physical feelings which we confuse and misinterpret as psychical assurances of a self distinct from the perceptions, volitions, or emotions which occupy, at the time, the field of consciousness. Thus we fancy that we are conscious of a self distinct from the fleeting feelings of the moment, whereas it is only a nervous or muscular strain which is experienced, and which is interpreted as an experience of a self. It is insisted that this is but one of the many by-products of consciousness, a phenomenon so constant and yet withal so colorless that it cannot be referred to any particular state of consciousness, to any definite idea, or feeling, or to any external object of perception; and therefore because of this very vagueness and indefiniteness it is believed to be the foundation and the unifying principle itself of consciousness.

As an illustration of this theory, the

following experience of Professor James will no doubt prove of interest: "It is difficult for me to detect in mental activity any purely spiritual element at all. Whenever my introspective glance succeeds in turning around quickly enough to catch one of these manifestations of spontaneity in the act, all it can ever feel distinctly is some bodily process, for the most part taking place within the head. I cannot think in visual terms, for example, without feeling a fluctuating play of pressures, convergences, divergences, and accommodations in my eyeballs. In reasoning, I find that I am apt to have a kind of vaguely localized diagram in my mind, with the various fractional objects of the thought disposed at particular points thereof; and the oscillations of my attention from one of them to another are most distinctly felt as alternations of direction in movements occurring inside the head. In consenting and negating, and in making a mental effort, the movements seem more complex, and I find them harder to describe. The opening and closing of the glottis play a great part in these operations, and, less distinctly, the movements of the soft palate, etc., shutting off the posterior nares from the mouth. My glottis is like a sensitive valve, intercepting my breath instantaneously at every mental hesitation or felt aversion to the object of my thought, and as quickly opening to let the air pass through my throat and nose, the moment the repugnance is overcome. The feeling of the movement of this air is, in me, one strong ingredient of the feeling of assent. The movements of the muscles of the brow and eyelids also respond very sensitively to every fluctuation in the agreeableness or disagreeableness of what comes before my mind. In a sense, then, it may be truly said, that in one person at least the 'self of selves,' when carefully examined, is found to consist mainly of the collection of these peculiar motions in the head, or between the head and throat."[1]

By others it is urged that the self

---

[1] James, *Psychology*, Vol. I, pp. 300-301.

which is fancied is really nothing more nor less than the visual picture of one's person, rising in consciousness and barely recognized as a visual picture, and so, in a half dreamy way, it is confused with the idea of a distinct selfhood.

Others, again, refer the idea of self to the verbal idea of "I," "my," or "mine," which, inasmuch as it is no longer recognized as a verbal idea, lends itself readily to a like confusion, and a similar interpretation.

In reference to all of these explanations of the self, which explain by explaining away, it is well to call to mind the possibility of there being a real self, or a metaphysical self, in distinction from the empirical or psychological self. The consciousness of the empirical self, *i.e.* the self evidenced by these physiological accompaniments, may be mediated through a physical feeling, or a visual or verbal idea; and yet, this does not preclude the possibility of the real self underlying all of these manifestations of the empirical self. The Greeks drew a similar distinction between the ψύχη, the psychological self, and the νοῦς, the rational self. There is a like distinction in the German between *Seele* and *Geist*. The soul, the νοῦς, the *Geist*, is something more than conscious states; it is, in the words of Dr. Martineau, "the *reflective knowledge* of having such states."[1]

It may be well at this point to recall Hume's famous paragraph concerning the impossibility of there being any such thing as a distinct self: —

"For my part, when I enter most intimately into what I call *myself*, I always stumble on some particular perception or other of heat or cold, light or shade, love or hatred, pain or pleasure. I never can catch *myself* at any time without a perception, and never can observe anything but the perception. When my perceptions are removed for any time, as by sound sleep, so long am I insensible of *myself*, and may truly be said not to exist. And were all my perceptions removed by

[1] Martineau, *A Study of Religion*, Vol. II, p. 190.

death, and could I neither think, nor feel, nor see, nor love, nor hate after the dissolution of my body, I should be entirely annihilated; nor do I conceive what is farther requisite to make me a perfect nonentity. If any one, upon serious and unprejudiced reflection, thinks he has a different notion of *himself*, I must confess I can reason no longer with him. All I can allow him is, that he may be in the right as well as I, and that we are essentially different in this particular. He may, perhaps, perceive something simple and continued which he calls *himself;* though I am certain there is no such principle in me. But, setting aside some metaphysicians of this kind, I may venture to affirm of the rest of mankind that they are *nothing but a bundle or collection of different* perceptions which succeed each other with an inconceivable rapidity, and are in a perpetual flux and movement."[1]

Hume may not be able to find the self as object, but in the very language which

---

[1] *Treatise on Human Nature,* Vol. I, Pt. iv, sec. 6.

he uses he seems to be vaguely aware of the self as subject. There is a self consciously striving to find the self. The self which is searching is implied even in the confession of the elusiveness of the self which is sought for. Hume, moreover, makes an unreasonable demand in insisting that the self, if discovered, must be found stripped of all its activities. The self can never be revealed in its naked state. We naturally expect it to appear clothed in its attributes, and it is to be recognized through the manifestations of its own nature, which are the varied phenomena of consciousness. Man may be regarded as a bundle of perceptions, but that which unites the perceptions and holds together the bundle, must be something more than the sum of the perceptions themselves. The discrete parts do not unite themselves, but remain discrete parts, unless we conceive of a unifying principle which integrates the separate parts into one systematic whole.

It is urged, moreover, that the unity of our mental states is provided for by

THE PROBLEM OF MIND

the law of the association of ideas, inasmuch as every idea present in consciousness is capable of calling up another idea or ideas which are associated with it by similarity, contiguity, cause and effect, or by some kindred relation. It is true that a certain unity is thus attained, but the scenes are shifted so rapidly on the stage of consciousness that we have a series of unified states rather than an underlying unity which perdures through all states, and to which all must be directly related, however diverse they may be. I may have an experience A, a definite state of consciousness which suggests B, and B in turn suggests C, and so on to D, E, F, G, etc. There is a connecting link of association between consecutive terms at any given point in the series. But A may be related to B through an association of A with a part of B. A totally different part of B may be associated with C. If this is the case, the continuity of relation between A and C is broken. As the series increases, the impossibility of detecting the underlying unity of association between A and some far removed term in the series, or between an experience of last year, or even of yesterday, and the present moment of consciousness, is apparent. The necessity, therefore, of an identical centre of reference for all states of consciousness, however widely separated and disparate, forces itself upon us. In this representation, the relation of ideas to each other has been regarded as a chain or a series of simply connected terms, whereas, in fact, the true representation of our states of consciousness is that of an extremely complex web of interrelated ideas at any one given instant of time. This complexity increases the difficulty of regarding the conscious underlying unity experienced throughout the manifold variety of life's experience, as a mere unity of similarity which associated ideas bear to one another. Paulsen feels this when he defines the soul as a "plurality of psychical experiences comprehended into the unity of consciousness in a manner not further definable."[1]

[1] Paulsen, *Introduction to Philosophy*, p. 129.

In this definition there is a recognition of the fact that the self must be something more than the sum of the conscious states of experience, and that a unity is necessary in which these several states may be merged, even though the precise nature of that unity may not be further defined. Whatever the nature of that unity may be, it certainly is something more than an association of ideas, which can mean only the logical and orderly relation of ideas. Underlying all such relations there is need of a unifying self.

The testimony of Kant, and of Green, to the truth of this doctrine is found in a very forcible statement of Professor Green: "We have followed him (*i.e.* Kant) also, as we believe every one must who has once faced the question, in maintaining that a single active self-conscious principle, by whatever name it be called, is necessary to constitute a world of experience, as the condition under which alone phenomena, *i.e.* appearances to consciousness, can be related to each other in a single universe."[1]

From the point of view of genetic psychology, that is, the special inquiry concerning the beginnings and development of mental life, it is urged that there is a gradual evolution from simple to increasingly complex states of consciousness throughout all the successive stages of progressive psychical experiences; and that, therefore, the idea of a separate permanent self is incongruous to this conception of the constant change and the shifting scenes of our inner life. Such a development, however, does not seem necessarily to preclude the idea of an original nucleus of growth which preserves its own identity amid the indefinite variety of conscious states, and which, at the same time, acts as a unifying principle in coördinating all the several stages of development within the sphere of a permanent personality.

The Intellectualists and Voluntaryists. — We come now to a second problem

[1] Green, *Prolegomena to Ethics*, § 38.

within the domain of philosophical psychology, as to the primary and essential nature of consciousness. Is consciousness to be regarded as essentially intellect, or as will? This question gives rise to two schools. The intellectualist insists that the processes of perception, conception, judgment, inference, etc., constitute the foundation of all other mental experiences. On the other hand, the theory of voluntaryism would find the beginnings of mental life in the crude phenomena of will, in appetites seeking gratification, in desires seeking satisfaction, in the interminable striving and struggling which characterize all forms of life from the lowest to the highest.

Intellectualism received a very hearty support from Descartes, who emphasized the rational as the primal element of mind; in this he was followed by Spinoza and Leibniz. Later, Herbart, as one of the prominent articles of his creed, regarded ideas as primary, whose attraction and repulsion, after the analogy of material bodies, result in desire, feeling, and will.

On the other hand, Schopenhauer is the chief champion of the school of voluntaryism. He insisted that the underlying and controlling principle in all mental life was the will to live; and that all other mental experiences, either directly or indirectly, may be reduced to this as the original source of them all. The tendency, to-day, among philosophical thinkers, is to magnify the importance of the will, and this because it is urged that in the will there is a possible point where the forces of nature and the forces of mind may unite. If matter can be reduced to force, and mind to will, then it is maintained the synthesis of material force and mental effort under the category of the will may not be wholly visionary.

In reference to the question of the primacy of the will or of the intellect, it seems that the truth may most probably lie in the direction of Lotze's position that neither to the intellect nor to the will is primacy to be conceded, but that they are to be regarded as coördinate powers of the mind.

CHAPTER VI

THE PROBLEM OF KNOWLEDGE
("EPISTEMOLOGY")

OF the general problems of mind, there is one special problem, whose discussion forms a distinct discipline in philosophy, namely, the problem of knowledge, or epistemology. This problem, which, in modern philosophy, was started by Locke in 1690, presents a twofold aspect, first, respecting the source of our knowledge, and, second, respecting its nature.

As to the former question, concerning the origin of knowledge, there are two views, indicating opposite tendencies in thought, known as rationalism and empiricism.

Rationalism. — The former insists that the source of all knowledge is primarily in the mind, inasmuch as there are certain fundamental principles of which the mind is immediately aware, and which give form and system to the crude materials of sensation, and which, therefore, so far forth, modify and condition all experience. Such a view allows as primal elements of knowledge the original data given through sense-perception. It only insists that such data are not the sole source of knowledge, but that the mind also furnishes its own contributing factors to the complete result. For, it is held that the mind does not simply receive the impressions of the outer world, as though they were photographed upon a sensitive plate. The mind is regarded as active and not passive in the act of perception. The mind stamps the raw material of the senses with its own die, gives a character to that which would be merely a confused blending of chaotic sensations and automatic reactions, and which would lack wholly that orderly arrangement which characterizes our world of perceptions, ideas, and feelings. These controlling principles of the mind which, it is held, give form to the crude data of perception, are such general ideas as those of time, of space, of causation, of logical relation, and similar ideas which are regarded as of an *a priori* nature, to distinguish them from purely *a posteriori* knowledge. The former phrase refers, as has been before indicated, to knowledge which is prior to and conditions experience; the latter expression refers to knowledge which is solely the result of experience.

Empiricism. — We will now consider the theory which refers all knowledge to experience as its source, namely, empiricism. If such experience, as some hold, is essentially and solely the product of sensations received in consciousness, then it is known as the theory of sensationalism; of which form of empiricism, the brilliant French philosopher, Condillac, is an eminent representative. The key-note of empiricism is found in Locke's oft-repeated and oft-quoted phrase, occurring in his *Essay on Human Understanding*, "No innate ideas." The Empiricist holds that the mind is a *tabula rasa*, a surface smooth and clean, impressionable to the various sensory stimulations which write upon it the records of experience. The adherents of this doctrine very stoutly maintain that the so-called innate ideas, when subjected to the nearer scrutiny of a critical analysis, will be found reducible to simpler elements, which are manifestly the product of experience. Our idea of causation, it is insisted, is not an intuitive possession, but it has grown with our growth, through repeated observations of nature, which indicate an invariability and uniformity which we unconsciously generalize into an all-embracing formula of universal causation. When it is objected that even a small child gives evidence of possessing general ideas, out of all proportion in point of completeness to the extreme brevity of its limited experience, the reply is made, that the seemingly original mental possessions of the child, which its individual experience is utterly inadequate to account for, may nevertheless be explained by a race experience which the child inherits and which in its dawning consciousness appears as intuitive knowledge.

The distinction between rationalism and empiricism marks one of the chief points of difference between the continental and the British philosophers. Of the rationalistic school we have Descartes, Spinoza, and Leibniz as the chief representatives, while of the school of Empiricism are found Locke, Hume, and John Stuart Mill.

The Critical School. — Kant, as a representative of the so-called critical school, insisted upon the empirical origin of the gross material elements of knowledge through the avenues of the senses, but, on the other hand, upon the rationalistic origin of the same as regards the formal element, which is manifested in the constructive function of the mind. Kant expressed this thought in his famous doctrine: "Macht zwar Verstand die Natur, aber er schafft sie nicht." "The understanding constructs nature, but does not create it." The crude data of nature the mind fashions into ideas through its own thought functions. The mind is an architect, though not the creator of thought.

Positivism. — A modified form of empiricism is that which is known as positivism, a philosophic system associated with the name of its founder, August Comte, born in 1789. He insisted upon the positive facts of experience, the facts which form the subject matter of science, as the sole basis of our knowledge. In reference to all speculation concerning theories which such facts may suggest, he declares that man must remain agnostic. Comte, moreover, maintained that mankind passes through certain phases of thought in an upward development. These phases are three in number, the theological, the metaphysical, and the positive, the latter being the final goal of knowledge. In the first stage, Comte says, phenomena are regarded as caused by wills similar to ours; the progress of thought in this stage passes from a grossly superstitious fetichism, through polytheism, to the more refined form of monotheism. In the metaphysical stage, certain mental abstractions are held to constitute the power underlying all nature, such as the idea of force, of occult powers or virtues inherent in substances. In the third and advanced stage, Comte regards all knowledge as circumscribed by the general laws of science which have been experimentally determined, and which account for the sequence of phenomena, the measurement of their intensity, and all their quantitative relations, but which, however, are silent concerning the underlying ground of these phenomena, and their significance in the light of the purposes or ends which they subserve. The end of knowledge, according to Comte, is the more perfect systematization of the sciences, in which task all metaphysical presuppositions must be strenuously avoided. It is evident, however, that such procedure would leave no place for a philosophy of knowledge.

The Nature of Knowledge. — A second problem is the nature of knowledge as the expression of reality. In what way is our knowledge related to reality? In what sense is the inner world of consciousness a real world? It is of supreme importance that the student of philosophy should appreciate the nature of this problem, its many difficulties, and the main points at issue. To grasp appreciatively the difficulties of a problem, is the first step towards a solution. Let us, therefore, attempt a more detailed statement of this question, and the perplexities which arise in its wake.

Whatever our theory of the source of knowledge may be, we are constrained to recognize the senses as the organs of mediation between us and the external world. An outer stimulus is followed by a corresponding sensation. The sensation, however, is not the stimulus, however much it may be modified in transmission through the neural circuit to the brain; nor is the sensation a copy of the object which caused the stimulus. In vision, the outer stimulus is a vibratory movement in the ether, which is an invisible, highly elastic medium, filling all space and penetrating all bodies. The corresponding perception, however, is of an object possessing definite color, form, and location in space. The difference between the colors red and green, as regards the stimulus, is a difference in the number of vibrations in a second. In the finished perception it is a qualitative difference; as regards the stimulus, however, it is quantitative.

Here, in the problem of knowledge, emerges the old difficulty, which we found in the problem of ontology, the evident gap between physical antecedents and the psychical consequents. In the problem of knowledge, the question which confronts us is, how far the inner perception is a true representation of the world of reality. Are the relations of time and space, of cause and effect, merely projections of the mind upon the field of perception? May it not be true that our perceptions which seem to be perceptions of things are, after all, only mental experiences which have no corresponding reality, or a reality different from our mind's representation of it? May it not be possible even that the world of experience manifested in consciousness as a world of order, of law, of harmony, and of beauty, is a work solely of the constructive processes of the mind, so that a chaos without is transmuted into a cosmos within, as irregular, broken bits of glass in a kaleidoscope appear to the viewing eye as elaborate designs, accurately proportioned and exquisitely colored? We find these difficulties graphically portrayed in the celebrated allegory of Plato: —

"'Let me show you, in a figure, how far our nature is enlightened or unenlightened: Behold! human beings living in an underground den, which has a mouth open towards the light, and reaching all along the den; they have been here from their childhood, and have their legs and necks chained so that they cannot move, and can only see before them; for the chains are arranged in such a manner as to prevent them from turning round their heads. Above and behind them the light of a fire is blazing at a distance, and between the fire and the prisoners there is a raised way; and you will see, if you look, a low wall built along the way, like the screen which marionette players have in front of them, over which they show the puppets.'

"'I see.'

"'And do you see,' I said, 'men passing along the wall, some apparently talking and others silent, carrying vessels and statues and figures of animals, made of wood and stone and various materials, and which appear over the wall?'

"'You have shown me a strange image, and they are strange prisoners.'

"'Like ourselves,' I replied, 'and they see only their own shadows, or the shadows of one another, which the fire throws on the opposite wall of the cave?'

"'True,' he said; 'how could they see anything but the shadows, if they were never allowed to move their heads?'

"'And of the objects which are being carried in like manner they would only see the shadows?'

"'Yes,' he said.

"'And if they were able to talk with

one another, would they not suppose that they were naming what was actually before them?'

"'Very true.'

"'And suppose, further, that the prison had an echo which came from the other side, would they not be sure to fancy that the voice which they heard was that of a passing shadow?'

"'No question,' he replied.

"'Beyond question,' I said, 'the truth would be to them just nothing but the shadows of the images.'"[1]

This is the problem, therefore, — whether our world is made up of shadows of images merely, or whether it is a world of reality? The answer to this question may be of a psychological, logical, or metaphysical nature. The psychological answer is satisfied with an accurate account of the process by which the outer world becomes an object of consciousness, tracing the external stimuli through the nerve channels to the brain

The Republic, VII, 514.

tracts and to the final mental reaction in consciousness. From the standpoint of special psychology, no other answer seems relevant.

The logical answer is, that the world within and the world without are corresponding worlds, so that there can be a constant basis of reference. The idea of invariability, as characterizing the world of experience, is a necessary logical postulate, for, without it, inference would be impossible. The world, as we know it, must be a world of uniformity, or else it would be impossible to reason, as we do in logical inference, from the functions of a part to the nature of the whole, or *vice versa.*

The metaphysical answers are two, forming the opposed schools of thought, realism and idealism.

Realism. — Realism, or, as it is generally styled, natural realism, is that theory which regards the world of perception as a true representation of the world without, and insists also that the world without has a real existence, and that its phenomena continue to manifest themselves in their physical actions and reactions even when the perceiving mind ceases to observe them.

Realism is of two kinds, a naïve, and a critical realism. The former is the result of a common-sense judgment which, without reflection, accepts a theory of crude dualism, and does not seek to go behind the appearance of an external world without and an internal world within. It accepts the facts, as they seem to be, from the standpoint of a practical mind which is but slightly introspective. Critical realism discriminates between the crude data of perception and the completed product to which the mind is a contributing factor which must be reckoned with in framing a theory of knowledge. It nevertheless maintains a dualism between mind and matter, although of a more refined type, and insists upon the reality of an objective world which is independent of the mind, which may or may not observe it.

The theory of realism is associated with

the Scottish school of philosophy, whose founder was Thomas Reid, followed by Oswald, Beattie, Dugald Stewart, and McCosh.

Idealism. — Idealism insists that the only world which is known to us is the world which appears in consciousness. Whether there is an external world corresponding, is a matter of surmise, but never of certainty.

One of the most eminent of the idealists, Bishop Berkeley, declared that nothing exists except as it is an object of perception. *Esse est percipi.* Locke had drawn the distinction between primary and secondary qualities of matter; the former, as extension, weight, etc., he regarded as objective qualities inhering in the object perceived; while the latter, the secondary qualities, as color, taste, smell, were subjective reactions and not qualities inherent in the object. Bishop Berkeley went a step farther, and said, that as the color red is an affection of the sensibilities and not resident in the object, so, also, form, weight, and force are all subjective constructions with no corresponding essences that can be regarded as constituting an object external to the subject, *i.e.* the perceiving self, or Ego. Hume carried Berkeley's argument a step farther still, in insisting that even the varied subjective manifestations appearing in consciousness were mere phenomena which possess no more trustworthy assurances of reality than do the phenomena of the world of matter. Hume pushed Berkeley's argument to the extreme of absolute scepticism.

Kant's phenomenalism is, in a way, a form of idealism in that he held that all things, whether material or mental, appear as mere phenomena, adding, however, that behind every phenomenon there must be a corresponding noumenon, that is, a real entity, referred to by Kant as the thing-in-itself to distinguish it from the thing-as-it-appears. This thing-in-itself, however, can never be known; it is the unknown quantity behind every phenomenon, the x of the equation of knowledge. In Lange's *History of Mate-*

rialism he cites Kant's doctrine in support of materialism, inasmuch as a denial of any reality that can be known leaves only the material appearances as the beginning and end of our knowledge. It must be noticed however, in passing, that Kant, in his *Critique of Practical Reason*, restores the world which, in his *Critique of Pure Reason*, he destroys. For Kant declares that in the intuitions of conscience, which are regulative of the will, that is, of the practical reason, there is evidence of a world of law and of order, which pure reason, unaided, is not able to prove. Kant assigns the primacy to the will and not to theoretical reason. It is the will, he urges, which is directly conscious of a law which imposes obligation and responsibility, and, therefore, so far forth, gives assurance that the world in which the will must fulfil its obligations must be an orderly, self-consistent, law-obeying world, or otherwise law, obligation, duty, obedience, could have no meaning and no field or scope for their activities.

Another form of idealism is the doctrine of the relativity of knowledge, as expressed by Sir William Hamilton. "Our whole knowledge of mind and of matter is relative — conditioned — relatively conditioned. Of things absolutely or in themselves, be they external, be they internal, we know nothing, or know them only as incognizable; and become aware of their incomprehensible existence only as this is indirectly and accidentally revealed to us through certain qualities related to our faculties of knowledge. All that we know is, therefore, phenomenal — phenomenal of the unknown."[1]

In Kant's phenomenalism as well as in Hamilton's doctrine of the relativity of knowledge we find the same assumption that, inasmuch as the object perceived sustains certain relations to the subject perceiving, therefore the perception itself must be colored by the nature of the subject, and the object of the perception therefore is not apprehended simply as it is in

---

[1] *Metaphysics*, I, p. 153.

itself. In other words, we look at Nature through the colored glasses of the Ego, the self. The Scottish philosophy, on the other hand, took the position, that while certain principles of our mind are operative in interpreting the nature and significance of every perception, we are nevertheless not deceived in such interpretation, inasmuch as there is a complete harmony between our nature and the nature of things.[1]

Prof. T. H. Green has further developed this idea and given it more exact philosophical expression in declaring that the spiritual principle in man, constituting the unity of his consciousness, is one with the spiritual principle in the world, which constitutes the law, the order, and the harmony of the universe. The synthesis of these principles in perception assures the reality of our world of knowledge.[2]

It must be observed, moreover, that our

---

[1] *On the Scottish Philosophy*, Andrew Seth, pp. 157-158.

[2] *Prolegomena to Ethics*, Book I, chap. i.

I

knowledge of phenomena is still real knowledge. There is a sneer in the phrase "mere phenomena" which is misleading. Objects in themselves and objects as they appear are not necessarily two distinct things. The thing-in-itself can manifest itself only through its attributes and through the manifold relations which these attributes sustain. It is a violent assumption that the thing-in-itself is one thing, and the manifestation of it something different, and therefore illusive. We are rather to think, with Hegel, that "thoughts do not stand between us and things shutting us from things, they rather shut us together with them." And it may be added, that the resulting knowledge is, therefore, of real things in a real world.

Absolute Idealism. — The doctrines of Hegel, as well as those of Fichte and Schelling, are a form of so-called absolute idealism. These doctrines, however they may differ in the details of representation, rest upon the identity hypothesis concerning the relation of matter to mind, which hypothesis, it will be recalled, regards matter and mind as related phases of one and the same underlying substance which unifies the two seemingly discrepant phenomena in their mutual interaction; moreover, absolute idealism considers this unifying substance to be a spiritual principle, which is at the same time the absolute principle of the universe. The antithesis of subject and object in the process of perception is resolved in a higher synthesis of a universal consciousness, of which subject and object are different modes. In Germany, the doctrines of Spinoza and a pantheistic philosophy were revived under the influence of Lessing and Herder. After Kant, we find Hegel, Fichte, and Schelling developing these ideas in various forms. Fichte emphasized the subjective, spiritual principle as the primal and all-comprehending essence of the universe which manifests itself in the various activities of the human will, conserving law, order, and moral force. On the other hand, Schelling insisted upon an objective idealism, as well as a subjective, the manifestation in nature of the spiritual principle, whereby the ideal finds expression in the concrete real, the two being essentially one. Hegel's idealism is a logical system based upon the proposition that the necessities of thought determine rigidly the necessities of being. His dictum is that the rational is the real. The necessary thought relations therefore determine a definite programme to which the actual phenomena of the universe, in their unfolding, conform. Everything that exists was originally an idea in the Divine Mind. The Absolute Being, or the Idea, as Hegel designates the supreme principle of all being, manifests Himself in nature, in man, in history, art, law, ethics, religion, and all the manifold phases of existence. The systems of absolute idealism, it will be seen, are essentially pantheistic, panlogistic, or pamphysical, according as there is emphasized severally the personal nature of the All-Being, or the nature of the same regarded as impersonal reason, or as a material force.

In the philosophy of Herbart, we find a natural reaction from the dogmas of Hegel; for he insists that things cannot be identified with thought, but that they exist independent of the reason which cognizes them. The business of philosophy, according to him therefore, is to seek a more exact and adequate formulation of the concepts which express the underlying principles of the different sciences. Herbart recognizes a number of distinct realities in the world, and these it is our duty to know and understand. The tendency of thought to react from an absolute idealism is a most natural one and has many illustrations; on the other hand, a tendency towards a crude realism, and a radical dualism, meets the same reactive tendency in the opposite direction. The truth must lie somewhere between the two extremes.

CHAPTER VII

THE PROBLEM OF REASON

THE normative sciences, logic, ethics, and æsthetics, form a single group in virtue of the common feature that each refers to a norm, or standard, by which reason, conduct, or taste is to be judged. We find ourselves in the realm of law; its interpretation and application constitute in this sphere the offices of philosophy.

Of the normative sciences, logic is the one which deals with the problem of reason. Reason may be regarded in the special significance of the term as equivalent to the process of reasoning, and therefore as synonymous with inference, one of the departments of logic proper. Reason, however, may have a more general and comprehensive meaning as synonymous with the understanding, and including the concept and the judgment as well as inference. The science of logic, therefore, embraces these three modes of thought, the concept, judgment, and inference.

The Concept. — Of these the concept is the simplest form; the judgment is a developed form of the concept, and inference, a further development of the judgment. Moreover, back of the concept there is still a simpler psychical phenomenon, namely, the percept which forms the foundation of the concept. The percept is the finished product in the process of perception. When a number of percepts are observed to possess certain common characteristics, the mind seizes upon these common marks and frames them into one general idea, which represents a class or a group of objects of which each separate percept in question stands as an individual example. After we have perceived a number of roses, we will find that the resulting percepts are distinctly different as regards size, color, fragrance, and many other qualities. Each individual rose preserves a marked individuality, and yet from the group of differing individual cases, the mind constructs a general idea of a rose which embodies the common marks, or general characteristic features, of all the roses which we have ever observed. The general idea is not visualized as a picture in the mind's field of vision; it is intellectually, not sensibly, discerned. The German word for concept, *Begriff*, gives the significance of the term more strikingly; it is the mind's *begreifen*, the grasping the common and essential characteristics of a class-idea, and holding them together. The concept, by itself however, is a floating idea in the mind, needing an anchorage to some definite and explicit form of thought which we find in the judgment. The judgment is the direct reference of a concept to reality; it is the saying something about the concept in the form of an assertion which may be either affirmative or negative. The judgment is a statement that the concept in the mind actually describes and represents the world of reality as we know it. The judgment, all metals are conductors, signifies that the attribute of conductivity is so essential to the integrity of our idea of a metal as to form one concept with it, to which reality in general must always correspond, to the extent that wherever in the world of reality we find a metal, we will always find the attribute of conductivity. While judgment is a *direct* reference of a concept to reality, inference, on the other hand, may be defined as an *indirect* reference of a concept to reality. I assert that a handful of black sand contains iron; I venture this assertion because I have held a magnet in close proximity, and immediately the sand particles attached themselves to it. My knowledge in such an experiment is gained indirectly and therefore is of the nature of inference; for that part of reality under investigation is characterized by me as containing iron by virtue of two judgments, and therefore discovered in a roundabout way. The one judgment is of a fact, that the magnet did actually attract the sand particles, and the other is a judgment of a universal nature, namely, that magnets will attract only substances of iron. Through these judgments, therefore, we reach, by an indirect process, the conclusion or inference that the sand in question contains iron particles.

The three divisions of logic, the concept, judgment, and inference, each present certain problems of general philosophical interest in addition to the more special problems of a distinctively logical nature.

The consideration of the theory of the concept suggests a question concerning the nature of the universal idea which a concept expresses, — that is, in such general ideas as rose, dog, man, in what sense may these terms be regarded as universals? It is an old controversy, this subject of the nature of universals, waged with much bitterness and tedium among the schoolmen of the middle ages.

There are three answers to this question, that of realism, of nominalism, and of conceptualism.

Realism. — In this connection, realism is used in quite a different sense from the term realism with which we are familiar in the problem of knowledge. The realist, as regards the nature of the universal, insisted that corresponding to every general class notion, there was a real being in which all the common marks which constituted the class characteristics were actually embodied. The general notion, man, therefore, would be incarnated in some essence possessing all the salient features by virtue of which man is man, and which exist therefore as an archetype of all mankind. The most eminent representative of this theory was Anselm. His famous argument on the being of God was based on realistic preconceptions. "When Anselm believed that with the help of the mere conception of God he could arrive at the proof of His existence, he exemplified in a typical manner the fundamental idea of realism which ascribed to conceptions without any regard to their genesis and basis in the human mind the character of truth, *i.e.* of Reality. It was on this ground alone that he could attempt to reason from the psychical to the metaphysical reality of the conception of God."[1]

From this quotation, it will be seen that the realist, in the discussion of the schoolmen, was a veritable idealist, according to the modern terminology in usage in the discussion of the theory of knowledge, for the scholastic realist maintained that reality could be found only in ideas.

Nominalism. — On the other hand, however, the nominalist insisted that the universal was merely a name, and that all the common attributes of a class gather round the name as a nucleus, and being thus held together in common verbal association, are presented to the mind, when occasion offers, through this verbal medium. Roscellinus is the chief representative of nominalism.

Conceptualism. — The conceptualist urged that the individuals of a class have more than the name in common; that they have the name plus the sig-

---

[1] Windelband, *A History of Philosophy*, p. 293.

nificance of which the name itself is a symbol. The mind's idea, the concept, is regarded by the conceptualist therefore as the universal; of this doctrine Abelard is the mediæval champion.

Plato's doctrine of ideas is often referred to as Platonic realism,— but realism however, in the scholastic significance of the word, and therefore actually an idealistic theory. According to Plato, every universal idea has a real counterpart in the world of reality. Commenting upon Platonism, Mr. Pater remarks:—

"It was like a recrudescence of polytheism in that abstract world; a return of many gods of Homer veiled now as abstract notions, Love, Fear, Confidence, and the like; and as such the modern anthropologist, our student of the natural history of man, would rank the Platonic theory as but a form of what he calls 'animism.' Animism, that tendency to locate the movements of a soul like our own in every object, almost in every circumstance, which impresses one with a sense of power, is a condition of mind, of which the simplest illustration is primitive man adoring, as a divine being endowed with will, the meteoric stone that came rushing from the sky. That condition 'survives,' however, in the negro, who thinks the discharging gun a living creature; as it survives also, more subtly, in the culture of Wordsworth and Shelley, for whom clouds and peaks are kindred spirits; in the pantheism of Goethe; and in Schelling, who formulates that pantheism as a philosophic, a Platonic theory, — such 'animistic' instinct was, certainly, a natural element in Plato's mental constitution,— the instinctive effort to find *anima*, the conditions of personality, in whatever preoccupied his mind."[1]

I have quoted from Mr. Pater somewhat at length in order to illustrate a tendency of thought which has characterized the ancient, mediæval, and modern philosophical speculations alike.

The Philosophy of Judgment. — The problem which arises in the theory of

---

[1] *Plato and Platonism*, Walter Pater, p. 153.

judgment is suggested in the definition of judgment itself; judgment being the direct reference of the concept to reality, we are confronted with the familiar epistemological difficulty as to the precise nature of the relation of the idea in the mind to reality. The problem in its strictly logical significance is, however, somewhat simplified inasmuch as logic has to do only with the content of consciousness. A judgment asserts as true certain concepts; truth, in this connection, means a correspondence to facts, and the facts with which logic deals are the elements of reality as they appear in consciousness. They are thought-facts.

The so-called thing-in-itself is never an object of consciousness, and, therefore, the world of reality, of which our judgments testify, is the world as we know it. And this world is characterized by a uniform experience, so that we are convinced that there must be a universal validity in all relations once conclusively established and adequately formulated in our judgments. This universality may be described as an identity in the midst of differences, that is, the world of knowledge is indefinitely variable in its manifold manifestations, and yet throughout all the possible variations of experience there remain certain constants. These constants form the ground of our judgments; they are dependable, so that upon them we may build various thought structures, with the absolute confidence which is inspired by the conviction that we are logical creatures, and that our world of knowledge is a self-consistent, uniformly related whole. We believe, therefore, that our judgments once true will be found always true; in the midst of many shifting uncertainties, this, at least, is solid ground.

The Philosophy of Inference.— The problem which presents itself for consideration in the theory of inference relates to the ground upon which the inferential process is based. What is the warrant for a procedure in inference from something known to an assertion concerning the unknown? We found that the essence of inference lies in an indirect reference of a concept to reality; but what ground have we for an indirect reference of our ideas to a sphere of reality which does not lie directly within our ken? The answer to this question we may find in the nature of our body of knowledge considered as a whole. We must regard our knowledge in its totality as forming a system of interrelated and orderly connected parts, so that a knowledge of any part necessitates a knowledge of all its nearly related parts.

The known which is given in consciousness, and the unknown which is inferred, must so hang together that the one implies the other. From the seed, we infer a certain kind of flower, or of grain, which the future in time reveals, thereby verifying the early prophecy which was born of reason. Regarding, therefore, the world of our knowledge as a system of interrelated parts, the characteristic and essential features of the system must remain the same from time to time; otherwise inference would be impossible. These relations may be depended upon so far as they hold universally. The discovery of a truth, therefore, is the discovery of a relation which holds universally; and this is the significance of the phrase, once true, always true. A fact, however, is a particular happening without reference to the conditions which produced it, and with no analysis of their nature so as to reveal the existing relations of a universal character which lie at the basis of the fact in question. A formulation of these universal relations constitutes the general truth of which the fact is a concrete particular example.

Deduction and Induction. — In inference, therefore, when we have given a knowledge of the universal relations which characterize any system as it always appears in consciousness, then we may infer certain particular facts which such universal relations necessitate. Such a process of reasoning is known as deduction. This is the logic of Aristotle. If, on the other hand, however, we have given a number of facts, and proceed from them to infer the universal characteristics and general features of the system in which alone such facts could possibly inhere, then we have a process of inference known as induction. Francis Bacon is the father of inductive logic. If from our knowledge of the planetary system we infer the particular position of sun, moon, and earth at any given time, as in the calculation of an eclipse, the procedure is deductive. But, if we investigate the several movements of the different planets, and from them infer the necessary nature of the system of which they are parts, we have the process of induction.

The Problem of Causation. — The universal relations existing between parts of one and the same harmonious system, and furnishing a basis for our inferences, are largely the relations of cause and effect. The doctrine of causation presents a problem of general philosophical interest. This problem is virtually a special case of the general problem concerning the empirical, or the *a priori* origin of knowledge. Is the idea of causation the result of experience or is it prior to experience? Such is the problem of causation, in its general philosophical significance; in its more strictly logical bearings, the essential question seems to be, "Is there an element of invariability in causation?" The invariability of the cause and effect relation, that like antecedents under precisely the same conditions produce like effects, alone makes inference possible. General philosophy may discuss the question as to the origin of our assurances of the existence of such a constant element in the world of experience; that is, whether our belief in the uniformity of nature and consciousness arises empirically or in an *a priori* manner. Logic, however, demands only that the fact of this invariability be assured.

Reasoning, if it is possible at all, must assume as a fundamental postulate, therefore, that nature, as it is represented in our world of knowledge, is uniform and self-consistent throughout.

Logic and Epistemology.— In the theory of logic, the problems are largely those which confront us in the theory of knowledge. Indeed, with some philosophical writers, especially in recent times, the study of logic has been merged in the science of epistemology. Logic, however, may not be thus absorbed. It is related most intimately to epistemology, but retains its individual nature as a distinct philosophical discipline. Logic in its scope embraces a large field which is foreign to the general subject matter of epistemology; for logic is a technical science, treating not merely the philosophical ground of the conceptual and inferential processes, but developing a method of discovering and formulating universal relations, which, in turn, may be applied to the determination of particular problems in concrete cases. Logic provides also, on its practical side, scientific methods of investigation, rules of experimentation, and laws which govern the interpretation of results. There is consequently not only a philosophy of our reasoning powers, there is an art of reasoning as well.

CHAPTER VIII

THE PROBLEM OF CONSCIENCE
("ETHICS")

THE problem of conscience falls within the province of ethics, and is concerned with the inquiry as to the origin and nature of the principles which underlie right conduct. The term, Ethics, is from the Greek, ἠθικά, meaning customs, or manners. The term, morals, is from the Latin *mores*, which has a like signification; so also, the German word for morals, *Sitten*. In the growth of language, the general meaning of morals has become restricted so as to apply solely to the specific sphere of commendable customs. A radical distinction between customs right and wrong has thus become crystallized in language. The import of this is significant, for it indicates a natural trend of thought which differentiates conduct as right and wrong. The question naturally suggests itself, What is the ground of this distinction? A philosophic spirit refuses to accept this distinction as a matter-of-course or to regard it as one of the commonplaces of our mental store, which is to be assumed and not explained. A reason for this classification of conduct is naturally demanded, and in the various attempts to render a satisfactory account of so evident and universal a distinction, two tendencies of thought are evident. The one would explain the recognized difference between right and wrong conduct as an immediate deliverance of consciousness; that is, knowledge which is intuitively discerned. The opposed school of thought would insist that such a distinction is obviously the outcome of experience, and the gradual growth of an ethical consciousness which is capable of discerning ever more clearly between right and wrong, the good and the evil. We are, therefore, at the very threshold of ethical inquiry, confronted with the general problem of knowledge in one of its special phases, namely:

Is the source of knowledge to be regarded as *a priori* or *a posteriori?* intuitive or empirical? Here the problem concerns the ethical consciousness solely, and not consciousness in general.

The *a priori* point of view leads to certain characteristic conclusions, as also, on the other hand, the empirical point of view. One's general philosophical position, therefore, will naturally determine in advance the lines of attempted solution as regards the more special problem which arises in the sphere of ethics. As to the origin of the ethical concept, there are four distinct schools of thought: the intuitional, transcendental, utilitarian, and evolutional. Of these, the two first trace the ethical ideas, which are the present possession of mankind, to an *a priori* source; the two last refer the same to an empirical source.

The intuitional position regards the ethical concept of the right in distinction from the wrong as innate, and prior to the knowledge which is derived from experience, and therefore as superior to, and regulative of, the suggestions of sense in appetite, passion, or desire. The transcendental theory, or transcendental evolution, insists that there is a gradual unfolding of the ethical concept in the development of mental life, but that this evolution, however, has proceeded from certain fundamental and germinal ideas of consciousness, and not from the data of sense-perception. The universal consciousness comes to its gradual manifestation in the developing conscience of each individual. This development is transcendental in the sense that it occurs in a sphere above the natural series of sensuous experiences. The utilitarian position regards all our ethical ideas as the result of an experience which indicates the kind of conduct which in times past has proved useful in producing pleasure and avoiding pain. The idea of utility, whence the name of the school, is thus associated with a pleasure-pain theory as to the ends of conduct, and the impulses to action. The evolutional theory, or the theory of natural evolution, as it is sometimes styled to distinguish it from transcendental evolution, differs from utilitarianism in insisting that the ideas of utility cannot form and develop in the brief lifetime of an individual, but necessitate a race experience which in the individual consciousness appears as a hereditary possession, but with the seeming nature and force of an intuition of right and wrong.

The above are the broad and general distinctions in ethical theory. There are, however, other questions which emerge within the bounds of the different schools themselves, and which arise out of the relations which these schools sustain to each other.

Intuitionalism. — The intuitional school is divided into a right and left wing according to the answer which is given to the question concerning the nature of our moral intuitions: Are they judgments of right and wrong, or are they feelings which discriminate between the right and wrong? Among the intuitionalists, therefore, we have this division, into the opposed camps of the intellectualists and the sentimentalists. The former say that we know the right as a matter of pure intellection; the latter, however, declare that we possess a faculty which is able to sense the right, and that just as we are able to appreciate the flavor of a fruit or the fragrance of a flower, so there is this extraordinary moral sense which divines the right, and appreciates its worth. The intellectualists are represented by the British moralists, Clarke, Cumberland, Cudworth, and Price; also by Kant. The sentimental school is represented by Adam Smith, Hutcheson, Shaftesbury, and Bishop Butler.

The tendency in modern writers of the intuitional school is to unite the cognitive and emotional elements so that the conscience is regarded as a synthesis of the two. This is the characteristic feature of Dr. Martineau's ethical system, in which conscience is represented as an arbiter of conflicting desires, so that, when the mind judges in favor of a higher impulse in the presence of a lower there is right action, but when the lower is judged superior in the presence of a higher impulse there is wrong action.

The strength of the intuitional position lies in its insistence upon an original concept of oughtness which renders the ethical ideal obligatory. That which is true to reason becomes law unto the will. Right is chosen for right's sake. The categorical imperative, to use Kant's famous phrase, becomes the corner-stone of the intuitional structure. An imperative which is categorical is a command uttered without reservation or condition; when duty lays upon us the burden of obligation, no reason need be assigned, no reward offered. It is the old-time rigorism of the Stoics. Kant has forcibly expressed this thought in his eloquent apostrophe:—

"O duty! Thou great, thou exalted name! Wondrous thought, that workest neither by fond insinuation, nor by flattery, nor by any threat, but merely by holding up thy naked law in the soul, and so extorting for thyself always reverence, if not obedience, before whom all appetites are dumb, however secretly they rebel! Whence thy original?"

The position, however, where the intuitionalist is especially exposed to attack, is his claim of universality for the ethical concept. For this concept being intuitive, it must follow that it is the common possession of mankind, and therefore must possess universal validity. In opposition to such a claim, it is urged that there is an evident diversity of opinion concerning moral judgments, and that the fact of moral progress from the crude ideas of the right in the savage mind to the highly refined moral sentiments and practices of a civilized community cannot be harmonized with an intuitive basis of morality. The intuitionalist's explanation of these evident difficulties is, in general, an application of a Kantian distinction to the problem in question; namely, as regards the form of the ethical concept, there are present certain constant and universal characteristics, but as to the precise content of the same in any special circumstance, there may be variations within certain limits. That we are under a moral law imposing obligation upon our wills, it is held we do not need to wait for experience to teach us; experience, however, does instruct us as to the appropriateness and the validity of applying such a law to concrete cases.

Transcendentalism. — The transcendental school of ethics is characterized by the general features of the larger philosophical system of which it is a part. That larger system regards the world, nature, man, history, science, art, religion, and, in a word, the totality of all the possible phases of being as the manifestation in continuous development of the universal reason, which is operative in and through all things. The outer form is the universe, the inner architectonic spirit is the creative and sustaining power of the supreme Being.

The moral consciousness of man is therefore to be regarded as one phase of the universal manifestation of the World-Spirit, the eternal consciousness. Among the many possible causes of conduct at any one time in a man's experience, there is always one which is preëminently the best because it perfectly mirrors the mind of the absolute spirit. It is the privilege as well as the duty of the individual to know and to realize this best always and under all circumstances, and so fulfil in his history the complete potential of his being. The ethical doctrine of this school, in the words of Hegel, is, "Be a person, and respect others as persons," or, as it is otherwise expressed, as the ideal of "self-realization"; that is, make the most and best of self to the full measure of one's possibilities. This doctrine is sometimes styled very appropriately the theory of perfection. The duty, however, of perfecting oneself is complemented by the duty which is owing to one's fellows. Man is to develop his own personality to the full, and, in the doing of it, give scope and play to the development of other personalities which may be associated with him in life's interests and activities. In this theory, the duties owing to self and the duties owing to others, are coördinated by the profound principle, that each individual consciousness is a part of the eternal consciousness, and that, therefore, we are one with our fellows by virtue of a common relation to the central source of life and thought. Under this aspect, the phrase, the solidarity of mankind, takes on a new and deeper significance. In the spirit of the transcendental theory of ethics, Professor Green has summarized the content of the ethical ideal as a "will to know what is true, to make what is beautiful, to endure pain and fear, to resist the allurements of pleasure in the interests of some form of society."

There is a danger in this theory, however, despite its high ideal, that the self which is to be realized, being a manifestation solely of the eternal consciousness, may prove to be not a real self with a distinct individuality, but only the semblance of a separate personality, which is to be reabsorbed in the Absolute. The command, therefore, to realize self cannot be a real command if there

THE PROBLEM OF CONSCIENCE 145

is not a real self to whom it can be addressed.

Utilitarianism. — The school of utilitarianism is concerned with the question of the good rather than the question of the right. What kind of conduct will produce a real and lasting good? Such a question leads one into the sphere of a philosophy of pleasure. The foundation of such a philosophy must be discovered in the nature of that kind of pleasure whose realization characterizes normal conduct.

The earliest form of the pleasure theory of life is found in the ancient Greek philosophical system known as Cyrenaicism, whose chief representative, Aristippus, taught that the end of conduct solely desirable was that which could be realized in the sphere of the sensibilities. Pleasure, with him, meant the pleasures of comfort and ease, of gratified appetite, and satisfied desire. It is the crudest form of the pleasure theory, known as pure hedonism, a term derived from the Greek ἡδονή, pleasure.

A more serious consideration, however,

forced itself upon the Greek mind. Epicurus regarded pleasure as an idea which must be refined in the crucible of reason. He insisted, therefore, that not all pleasures should be indiscriminately sought after as the impulse of the fleeting present might dictate, but only those pleasures which experience proves will leave no painful after-effects in their train, and which are wisely tempered by moderation. In short, the doctrine of Epicurus was, that the pursuit of pleasure must be guided by prudence. This idea became the fundamental article of belief in the early English utilitarianism as represented by Hobbes. Ethics is thus reduced to a "calculus of pleasure" from the standpoint of the individual, and is known as egoistic utilitarianism, or egoistic hedonism. There was still a further differentiation as urged by Jeremy Bentham, which regards the pleasure to be sought in conduct as that which is conducive to the greatest happiness of the greatest number, and in this form the theory is known as altruistic hedonism, or altruistic utilitarianism. Bentham's fundamental conception of the relation of man to society was expressed in the principle that "every man should count for one, and no one for more than one.". The political discussions of the day concerning the rights of man no doubt contributed to the formulation of this dictum.

A further contribution to the theory of utilitarianism we find in the writings of John Stuart Mill. He insists that in estimating the worth of any pleasure, one must consider not only the quantity of pleasure which may accrue either to the individual or to society, but also the quality of the pleasure as well, inasmuch as there is among pleasures a rank of nature. This qualitative difference, insisted upon by Mill, constituted a modification of the utilitarian concept so radical that Mill has been very severely censured as a recreant to the sanctioned traditions of the utilitarian school. For the ethical concept, reduced to its lowest terms as experiences of pleasure and pain, may be determined in a quantitative manner by a purely psychological analysis, but psychological methods of interpreting experience cannot estimate differences of a qualitative nature, or determine the comparative worth of two pleasures upon a basis merely of quantitative value. A distinction between kinds of pleasure, as high or low, implies in itself a qualitative standard of comparison, that is, an ideal having certain constant and universal characteristics, and this conception brings utilitarianism, in its most refined form, within the borderland at least, of the intuitional territory.

The presence of these qualitative differences among our various pleasures is implied in the expression, eudæmonism,— a term which is used in contrast with hedonism. The former signifies happiness in its most comprehensive sense, so that the pleasures of the intellect, the satisfaction arising from moral approbation, the glow of feeling in the consciousness of duty performed, all are embraced within the one concept as well as the lower round of sensuous pleasures, which can be assessed simply in quantitative terms.

The Theory of Evolution. — This theory, in its ethical aspects, is a natural outgrowth of utilitarianism. The two theories have this in common: they both hold that the distinction between right and wrong is derived from an original distinction between pleasure-provoking and pain-producing phenomena. The point of departure, however, of the evolutionist is his insistence that the lifetime of an individual is too short to ground the association between pleasure giving and right actions, and that the derivation of the idea of right, from an original hedonistic source, is not as apparent as it would be if this derivation occurred in the brief span of an individual life. We have, therefore, Herbert Spencer's succinct account of the evolution of the ethical concept in the following paragraph: "Experiences of utility organized and consolidated during all past generations of the human race, have been producing nervous modifications, which, by continued transmission and accumulation, have become in us certain faculties of moral intuition, certain emotions responding to right and wrong conduct, which have no apparent basis in the individual experience of utility."[1]

The claim of the evolutionist, therefore, is that our knowledge of right and wrong is only a seemingly original possession of consciousness. It is urged, moreover, that our ancestors in immemorial ages found certain actions to be advantageous, in the long run, to the individual, or to the family, or to the tribe. Therefore, in the tribes where such actions became established customs, or *morals*, the advantages gained would result in the survival of the tribes when brought into competition or conflict with their less highly favored neighbors. The subsequent generations would inherit these life-conserving customs as predispositions of conduct, to which would attach themselves naturally certain sentiments of

[1] Spencer's Letter to Mill: Bain's *Mental and Moral Science*, p. 721.

fear, or reverence, or tribal loyalty; and thus there would develop a kind of mysterious sanction whose very indefiniteness would grow finally into the seemingly sacred and authoritative voice of conscience.

In the account of the evolution of conscience special stress is laid upon the duties owing to the tribe or to society. In the evolutional doctrine, society is regarded as an organism, of which the individual is a living cell, so that the health of the whole depends upon the healthful functioning of every part. Leslie Stephen, a follower of Spencer, has most strenuously championed the doctrine of the social factor as the essential characteristic of the ethical concept. He insists that the individual is one with the social organism, united with society of the past through the ties of heredity, and with society of the present through the manifold bonds of one's environment. "We are born," says Stephen, "not into a chaotic crowd, but into an organized army, and we must learn to keep step and rank, and to obey orders."

The evolutionist's view of the relation of man to his fellows differs substantially from that of the transcendentalist, in that the latter regards the bond of union, which is the basis of a common interest, as a spiritual fraternity rather than an organic tissue of vitally coördinated human cells. The bond of one is metaphysical; of the other, physical.

In the various controversies which have arisen among the several schools of ethics, there are two questions which possess general philosophic interest. One is the question concerning the freedom of the will; the other, concerning the relation of the ethical consciousness to the supreme Being of the universe.

Freedom of the Will. — The problem of the freedom of the will has given rise to two opposed schools of thought, known as the determinists and the indeterminists. The former hold that the will in any seeming choice is determined by preceding psychical states as antecedents. The mechanical sequences of the physical world find analogous relations in the mental world. Volition is held to be the result of motives which determine the course of action, both as to its nature and direction.

The indeterminist, on the other hand, contends that man has the consciousness of initiating action, and this, often in the face of opposing desires which are resisted and dominated; moreover, that the motive cannot be said to determine the self, the Ego, for the motive is merely the Ego in the act of desiring, and should not be considered as a separate force centre by which the Ego is affected.

The Kantian explanation of the point at issue in this protracted controversy between determinists and indeterminists consists of two propositions: the first will recommend itself at once to the man of common sense; the second perhaps will be appreciated only by the idealist of an ultra type. The former is, that man feels himself to be a responsible creature under a law of obligation, but that this feeling of responsibility can have significance only upon the supposition that the will is free.

The second part of the explanation is more metaphysical. Kant draws the distinction between the so-called phenomenal and noumenal aspects of the self, the Ego; that is, the mental phenomena, as feeling, desire, or volition, as they are discerned by us, seem to form a causal series subject to the law of an invariable sequence, but the real nature behind this phenomenal appearance, if adequately cognized, would disclose the real initiating power of the Ego. This explanation implies a self which is other than the sum of our conscious states. While every psychical state may be conceived as determined by previous psychical states, still, if there is a belief that there is a self which constructs these states into a unitary whole, then there is room for a self-determination which is a real freedom of the Ego in willing.

The general theory, therefore, which one holds concerning the nature of the Ego, will largely determine his special view regarding the freedom of the will; the materialist will naturally deny the possibility of such a freedom, and the pantheist will acknowledge only a seeming freedom whose reality is illusive.

Ethics and the Theistic Problem. — There is still the further problem to consider, whether in the moral consciousness there are intimations of the Divine Being. Such intimations are explicit in the writings of the intuitional and transcendental schools. The former affirms that in man's constitutional consciousness of a right for right's sake, of a law of duty commanding obedience, and of a responsive feeling of obligation, we find abundant evidence of a God; as Browning has said,

> "The truth in God's breast
> Lies trace for trace upon ours impressed."

The relation between man and God is further explained by the transcendentalist who insists that the individual consciousness is merely a manifestation of the universal consciousness. Thus God is reached through an apotheosis of man. The intuitionalist saves the autonomy of man by affirming that a relation exists between God and man so that there is mirrored in the consciousness of man the divine attributes as the ethical ideal, and yet at the same time man's individuality is not absorbed in the Absolute All.

In the systems of naturalism, that is, utilitarianism and utilitarian evolution, we find a theory of the origin of the ethical consciousness which seems to leave no place for, and to express no need of, a supreme Being. But, in whatever way the process of development may be explained without a supplementary hypothesis of a theistic character, nevertheless the inquiry forces itself upon our consideration concerning the end which this process is destined to attain; and this will lead to a profounder speculation, which may discern in the progress of evolution,

> "One God, one law, one element
> And one far-off divine event
> To which the whole creation moves."

Dr. Martineau has most graphically indicated the implied presence of God in the ethical concepts which may seem to be constructed upon other lines: "With a noble inconsistency, all the great writers, whose doctrine we have studied, betray the tenacious vitality of the intuitive consciousness of duty, throughout the very process of cutting away its philosophic roots; and Plato, in his 'divine wrath' at the tyrant flung into Tartarus; Malebranche, self-extinguished in the Absolute Holiness; Spinoza, lifted from the thraldom of passion into the freedom of Infinite Love; Comte, on his knees before the image of a Perfect Humanity, are touching witnesses to the undying fires of moral faith and aspiration."[1]

[1] *Types of Ethical Theory*, Vol. I, p. 512.

CHAPTER IX

THE PROBLEM OF POLITICAL OBLIGATION
("POLITICAL SCIENCE")

THE special problem which concerns man's political obligations is one which naturally grows out of a consideration of man's ethical relations in general. For, regarded as a moral creature, man is essentially a political animal, as Aristotle styled him. He lives, moves, and has his being in the society of his fellows, to whom he sustains manifold relations; whence there arise, on the one hand, various obligations, and, on the other, corresponding rights and prerogatives. Many of these relations find permanent form and expression in certain social institutions, such as the family, the church, or the state. These institutions are the external manifestation of the moral progress of mankind, and therefore an inquiry into their nature and development will reveal the fundamental principles of social ethics. This is especially true of the study of those social relations which centre in the state. The chief functions of the state seem to relate to law and to policy. Through law the sovereign power enjoins certain actions and prohibits others; through policy, on the other hand, wise measures of government are conceived which tend to conserve the public health and safety, and, at the same time, to assure substantial progress. Public policy is essentially practical; it has to do with questions of ways and means. It is an art rather than a science. It is therefore to the rise and growth of law that we naturally turn in order to discover fundamental principles of general philosophical import.

We find that jurisprudence, which is the science of law, is closely related to ethics, and yet distinctly differentiated. The law commands obedience in respect to the outer act alone. Such obedience may be enforced even when the inner spirit secretly rebels, or openly protests.

In ethics, however, that inner disposition which manifests itself in respect for the ethical ideal is all essential, and this the legal command is not able to affect. The philosophy of law is concerned with the question, why certain external acts come to be enforced by a sovereign power in a tribe, in a community, or in a state. In this general question, there seem to be implied three special questions possessing some philosophical interest. These special questions concern the origin of law, the warrant of sovereignty, and the province of the state's control.

The Origin of Law. — As to the origin of law, we find two conflicting theories; one insisting upon an *a priori*, and the other upon an empirical source. A like distinction holds here which we found to be of such fundamental significance in the discussion concerning the origin of the ethical concept. This similarity is not a mere coincidence, however, for, while the ethical concept refers to obligation in its general aspect, and the legal concept to obligation of a specific kind, it is, nevertheless, the philosophy of obligation, which is the object of inquiry in each. That which is conceived as the ground of the moral concept will determine one's conviction to a great extent concerning the ground of the legal concept. He who is convinced that the ethical concept has an *a priori* basis, will naturally hold a similar view in reference to that particular phase of the ethical concept which relates to obligations which have become definitely formulated in the law of the land. On the other hand, a belief in the empirical origin of duty will lead to a belief in the empirical origin of law. We know that in the developing social life, certain customs, *mores*, have become morals, that is, they are regarded as obligatory upon all and receive a certain social sanction; in a like manner certain customs also come to be regarded as of such vital import to the preservation and welfare of society as to associate with them certain coercive measures, having the force of a legal sanction. As in ethics, so in jurisprudence, a fundamental inquiry takes us back to these original customs, and the question concerning them is whether they can be traced to an *a priori* or an empirical source.

The *a priori* origin of law is designated by a time-honored phrase, *the law of nature*, or *jus naturale*, to use the law language of the Romans. The empirical origin of law is indicated by the phrase, *positive law*, or *jus civile*. The law of nature implies an ideal of right, or law as it ought to be; positive law refers solely to law as it is. The ideal and the actual are here opposed, and it is the same situation precisely which we met in the discussion as to whether ethics is the science of that which is, or of that which ought to be. The idea of a law of nature as the ground of all positive law may be best indicated perhaps by the two following quotations, — the first from an old Roman lawyer and the second from a German philosopher of modern times. Cicero says that the law of nature is "the highest reason implanted in nature, which commands those things which ought to be done, and prohibits those which ought not to be."[1] And Kant, in the same vein, has remarked: "What the law in any instance is, the jurisconsult can easily tell, but whether it is RIGHT or JUST that it should be so, is what he wants a criterion to determine. But this criterion can only then be found when, abandoning all *a posteriori* principles, he ascends to the sources of reason, and discovers on what all legislation whatsoever can alone be based; in which analysis positive law is doubtless a great help and guide. But laws founded singly on experience are like the mask in the fable — beautiful but hollow."[2]

In this theory of an original law of nature there is a combination of Greek and Roman elements. The Greek contribution to this idea was the ancient concept of the order and regularity of physical nature, which was afterwards extended so as to embrace the moral nature as well. The Roman contribution was the idea of order and uniformity which had been observed

[1] *De Legibus*, I. 6.
[2] *Metaphysics of Ethics*, p. 178.

among the various customs of different races, and which seemed to indicate a common origin in those principles which are grounded in a common human nature. In the Roman Jurisprudence, there was one law for the Roman citizen, the *jus civile*, and another, the *jus gentium*, for the alien who might appear as litigant in the Roman courts. The *jus gentium* was the natural result of the existing conditions of Roman polity, for the rights and prerogatives of the citizen did not pertain to the foreigner, and therefore there arose a system of legal decisions in the form of Prætorian edicts, which were based upon the principles common to the various legal codes of the surrounding peoples. This gave a mass of legal principles which were founded upon common customs, and which, because largely void of local and temporal coloring, were regarded as quite independent of any particular experience, and, therefore, as possessing the character of natural laws. In these edicts we find the first model of courts of equity. The original meaning of the term, equity, was that of a "levelling" process, or the reduction of the rights of man in general to a common basis of human nature. Hence the phrase, the rights of man, was early associated with that other watchword of the *a priori* school, the law of nature. These ideas have been made the basis for a philosophy of law from the time of the early Greek philosophy to the present; among the chief representatives of this school of political thought we find the Stoics, Cicero, Grotius, Trendelenburg, and Kant.

The idea of the law of nature appeared, however, in a distorted form in the writings of Hobbes, Rousseau, and the political philosophers of the French Revolution. The old formula was construed as indicating an original state of nature where an unrestrained liberty of the individual prevailed, and where each man did that which was right in his own eyes. Instead of an ideal principle of right and of liberty there was substituted a materialistic conception of a primitive society whose members were engaged in a struggle for existence under the impulse of unbridled desire, and of a license which had not yet known the meaning of law. The later German philosophers, as Kant, Hegel, Ahrens, Krause, and in England Prof. T. H. Green, have grounded the law of nature upon a more philosophical foundation in insisting upon the fundamental conception of personality as the source of all so-called natural rights. Man, as a person, is to be regarded not merely as a self-seeking individual, but as a member of a society of organically related persons, so that true self-realization is to be attained only through a self-sacrificing ministration to the general weal of the social organism. Natural rights, therefore, imply and necessitate corresponding duties, so coördinated that the good of each may redound to the good of all. The right which one may urge as truly inalienable is the right to realize oneself without let or hindrance in the performance of duties which devolve upon man as a participant in the communal life of a tribe or of a nation. This is a right which can be maintained not as against the social organism, but as making for its highest interests and welfare, as well as for the welfare and interests of the individual himself.

The exclusively empirical origin of law, on the other hand, has been stoutly urged. This theory, as might naturally have been expected, has received most enthusiastic support from the representatives of utilitarianism, Hobbes, Bentham, and Mill. It was Hume who first applied the doctrine of utilitarianism to a theory of political science. Moreover, the eminent jurist, Austin, a pronounced follower of Bentham, has based his system of jurisprudence upon utilitarian principles. From this point of view, law is regarded solely as the result of a wide experience concerning those customs which have proved conducive to the general good of past races, tribes, and nations. The prince of utilitarians is Macchiavelli who would not only sacrifice moral principles, but would even ignore the actually existing laws, if only the interests of the state might be conserved. His theory is utilitarianism pushed to the extreme; just as the doctrine of natural rights in the days of the French Revolution was the extreme and distorted form of the theory of natural law. Of Macchiavelli and his theory we have the following estimate by Bluntschli: "He has adorned an immoral and unjust policy, has put prudent counsel at the disposal of tyranny, and has thus helped to corrupt the political practice of the last three centuries."[1] It should, however, be conceded that utilitarian considerations must necessarily prove operative in questions of governmental policy, in legislation, and in all agitation and discussion concerning public affairs. In this respect political ethics differ from individual ethics, inasmuch as the individual ethic concerns the inner disposition, while the political ethic concerns necessarily the outer acts which can be enjoined or prohibited. Now the point of view of utilitarianism is such that the outer act and its consequences seem all important;

---

[1] *The Theory of the State*, Eng. Trans., p. 62.

the natural affinity, therefore, between political ethics and utilitarian considerations is evident. It is very strenuously urged, however, by those who favor some *a priori* foundation of legal principles, that utilitarianism without a check will run into wild Macchiavellianism, and that it needs precisely that conservative control which the idea of a natural law of right and of justice supplies.

It would be surprising, indeed, if there were not an application of the theory of evolution to the problem of the rise and growth of the legal concept, a theory corresponding in the main to the general theory of evolution as regards the ethical concept. Not only is there such a theory in fact, but it is forging more and more to the front, and proclaiming its doctrines with vigor and insistence. The evolutionist contends that states are not made, but grow, and that the law like language is the result of a gradual development. In this school, there are, on the one hand, those who emphasize the physical factors in this evolution, such as climate, geographical position, soil, water-ways, etc., and on the other hand, there are those who lay stress upon the mental factors, such as M. Fouillée styles "idea forces,"[1] and insist that they are all potent in modifying and determining the physical surroundings. The one is the evolution of naturalism, the other is essentially an idealistic evolution. Perhaps the most eminent representative of naturalistic evolution is Montesquieu, while Hegel valiantly defends a purely idealistic evolution, and contends that in the state institutions generally and in the law of the state particularly there is the external manifestation of the universal consciousness, which through the ages is thus gradually objectifying itself. The modern historical method of inquiry takes account both of the naturalistic and idealistic forces in the evolution of law. It is an inductive study of law as it is, and as it has been, in order to discover certain universal laws of tendency in the constitutions and codes of states. The founders

---

[1] Fouillée, *La Psychologie des idées forces.*

of the so-called historical school of jurists, Savigny and Puchta, emphasize the "idea forces" in the evolution of law, which they conceive as the gradual manifestation of the common consciousness of a people as it is disclosed in the detailed study of the comparative history of nations. In this connection, it is to be observed that the historical method is not necessarily at variance with an *a priori* basis of the idea of right and of liberty. Concerning this Bluntschli has said that "the old strife between these two methods has altogether ceased in Germany. Peace was made as early as 1840. Since then it is recognized on all sides that the experiences and phenomena of history must be illumined with the light of ideas, and that speculation is childish if it does not consider the real conditions of the nation's life."[1]

The Ground of Sovereignty. — There is a second question of general philosophical interest, concerning the warrant of sovereignty. Austin defines a sover-

[1] *The Theory of the State*, p. 70.

eign power as that "which is not in a habit of obedience to any determinate human superior, while it is itself the determinate and common superior to which the bulk of a subject society is in the habit of obedience."[1] By virtue of what authority can a portion of society compel obedience to its commands, while acknowledging no obedience to any power whatsoever? To this question there are several answers. The first is the theological view, that sovereign power has been delegated to the state by divine investiture. This idea was very vigorously challenged by the champions of the church prerogative. Thomas Aquinas, for example, contended that the state must be subordinated to the church, inasmuch as the church is the only institution which is divinely ordained. Dante coördinated the two powers, while Macchiavelli insisted upon the state's complete independence of the church. The writers of the Reformation period, moreover, declared that the state was divinely

---

[1] *Jurisprudence*, I, p. 171.

ordained, and that without the intervention of church dispensation. Two points seem to be pretty definitely settled: one is the entire organic independence of church and state, and the second is that sovereignty has not been a direct commission of the divine will. The latter is thoroughly compatible, however, with a theory of an indirect revelation of God's will to man in the constitution of human nature, and in the progressive experiences of mankind, so that in this sense the will of God may be regarded as the primal source of law, and, as such, the warrant for sovereign control.

Another theory traces sovereignty to might, pure and simple. Might is right, it is urged; and, therefore, there is no occasion for power to explain its own existence. This was substantially the theory of Spinoza, who identified *jus naturae* with *potentia naturae*, and insisted that the only thing which a state had no right to do was that which might in any respect lessen its power. The so-called analytical school of jurists, as Austin,

Holland, and Pollock, insist upon a like interpretation of the warrant of sovereignty. They hold, that after a careful analysis of positive law, the one essential idea which is revealed as an ultimate legal element, is the idea of a power which can compel obedience, and which can create in the social organism what Bagehot calls a "legal fibre."[1] The position of the analytical school has been criticised by the historical school of jurists generally, and in particular by Sir Henry Sumner Maine, who insists that by a mere process of abstraction the legal analysts reach a naked sovereignty stripped of all its coordinate attributes which are essential to the very integrity of the concept itself. He says of them that "they neglect the vast mass of influences which we may call, for shortness, moral, and which perpetually shapes, limits, or forbids the actual direction of the forces of society by its sovereign. . . . Just as it is possible to forget the existence of friction in nature,

Bagehot, *Physics and Politics*, p. 30.

and the reality of other motives in society except the desire to grow rich, so the pupil of Austin may be tempted to forget that there is more in actual sovereignty than force, and more in laws which are commands of sovereigns than can be got out of them by merely considering them as regulated force. . . . A despot with a disturbed brain is the sole conceivable example of such sovereignty."[1]

Still another account of the warrant of sovereignty is that of the social-contract theory, which has been so vigorously set forth in the writings of Hobbes and of Locke, and so brilliantly expounded in the impassioned utterances of Rousseau. This theory regards each individual as the possessor of inalienable rights, which he alone can delegate to another, and which no one may wrest from him. It is furthermore held that among primitive men, there was a recognition of the fact that individuals could live peaceably and harmoniously together in a clan, or tribe, only by making

---

[1] Maine, *Early History of Institutions*, pp. 359-361.

common concessions of the nature of a social contract whereby, on the one hand, certain rights of the individual would be freely surrendered, and, on the other, society as a whole would be obligated to guarantee the general good of all. The criticism of this theory is that it is not historical, inasmuch as the state has been a growth by imperceptible degrees, and not artificially founded by any formal contract. Moreover, this theory implies that man has existed with certain rights outside a society of his fellows, whereas by nature man is born into a plexus of social relations and cannot be rightly conceived as not possessing any such relations at all. The social-contract theory led to the idea of popular sovereignty which regarded law as an expression of the general will, and therefore as a corollary to this theory it was contended that the people had a right to destroy the sovereignty and annul the original contract, whenever the popular will might be consistently and constantly frustrated. This was the philosophy of the French Revolution. Here again the

German philosophy goes deeper than the French, for, while regarding the general will as the basis of sovereignty, it insists that such a basis does not itself rest upon any artificial contract but upon the solidarity which characterizes the common consciousness of man. This forms a natural foundation, and its expression in sovereign law is a natural manifestation. In accord with this latter view, Professor Green bases sovereign right upon the necessity of preserving the integrity both of the individual and the social personality. He says: "The claim or the right of the individual to have certain powers secured to him by society, and the counter-claim of society to exercise certain powers over the individual, alike rest on the fact that these powers are necessary to the fulfilment of man's vocation as a moral being, to an effectual self-devotion to the work of developing the perfect character in himself and others." [1]

The Province of State Control. — The

[1] Green, *Works*, Vol. II, p. 347.

third general question concerns the scope of the state's control. There are two opposed theories: one of ancient Greek origin, which emphasizes the prerogatives and power of the state, and the other, which reflects the eighteenth century spirit in insisting upon the rights of the individual as against the sovereignty of the state. It is social atomism opposed to the social organism. The theory of individualism in its extreme form leads to anarchy, which is the reduction of governmental functions to zero; the theory which magnifies the society at the expense of the individual, leads logically to socialism, which insists that society is to take charge of the individual and is itself to determine how he shall be trained, what he is fitted to undertake, and what he has earned by his effort.

As to the end of government there are two tendencies to be noted: one materialistic, which regards the sole function of government to be the maintenance of order and the repression of crime, and the other, which is idealistic, takes into account the ideas of humanity, as religion, science, and art. Is there a place for the so-called *Kulturstaat?* Should the state by enactment attempt to be the guardian of culture? Many who feel the yoke of government are clamorous for a *laissez faire* policy, less legislation, less governmental interference, let the laws of supply and demand, of competition, of invention, and of imitation, work out the salvation of the race. On the other hand it is urged that the state must take active measures to promote the public welfare both directly and indirectly. Compulsory education, for instance, only indirectly affects the public weal, and yet it is maintained that it is essential to public health and public safety. The mean may perhaps be attained by striving in all legislation to preserve the personality of each individual regarded as a contributor to the general good; and this, in two respects, to provide for the full exercise and development of each personality without over-restraint, and yet, on the other hand, to avoid dispensing that kind of help which diminishes self-respect and paralyzes effort. The idea of a paternal government implies that its members fail to possess those elements of personality which constitute a vigorous manhood, and give power and prestige to the state which is able to develop them. Here again we see that the idea of a personality which is not merely individual, but also social, reconciles the two conflicting ideas of socialism and individualism under one concept

CHAPTER X

THE PROBLEM OF THE SENSE OF BEAUTY
("ÆSTHETICS")

IN the sphere of æsthetics there are several problems of general philosophical interest. The term *æsthetics* is one which was first used by Baumgarten in his *Æsthetica*, published in 1750. The word is derived from the Greek, αἰσθάνομαι, to perceive through the senses; hence from its derivation it means a study of the sensibilities; not, however, of the sensibilities in general, but only of those feelings which are accompanied by appreciation of the beautiful either in nature or in art. The question at once suggests itself, "What is the beautiful?" To define beauty in clear and adequate terms is indeed a most difficult task. There is so great a diversity of opinion as to the essentials of beauty that the matter of simple definition is the first and perhaps the most serious problem which the philosophy of æsthetics presents. The difficulty lies in the fact that the consciousness of beauty is so simple and so common an experience as to baffle all attempts to analyze the resulting concept into any simpler elements. A concept which is framed from cognitive or intellectual elements is naturally more definite and clean cut than a concept composed of emotional elements. Goethe, with a poet's sensitive appreciation of the fugitive nature of our feelings, has expressed the conviction that "beauty is inexplicable, it is a hovering and glittering shadow, whose outline eludes the grasp of a definition."

Another difficulty in reference to the concept of beauty confronts us when we attempt to define the sphere in which beauty can be said essentially to reside. Is beauty a subjective state, a pleasurable feeling merely which objects produce in consciousness? or is beauty inherent as well in the objects themselves, so that the experienced pleasure within may be regarded as a reflection of the indwelling beauty without? In the latter case the final judgment concerning the beautiful must be regarded as the resultant of the qualities of the object observed, and of the reactive sensibility of the observer. It will be readily recognized that the fundamental problem in the theory of knowledge emerges here in the sphere of æsthetics, namely, the relation of that which is within consciousness to reality. Amidst these many difficulties there seems to be one characteristic of beauty, the truth of which we may assume without further discussion; that the consciousness of the beautiful is always a judgment of valuation. Associated with the idea of the beautiful there is always the idea of worth or of appreciation. This places the æsthetic judgment in the same class with the moral and logical judgments. All three recognize a certain ideal with which the concrete experience in each case is compared, and a resulting evaluation of the experience constitutes the judgment of morals, or of reason, or of taste.

"Beauty, Good, and Knowledge are three sisters
That dote upon each other, friends to man,
Living together under the same roof, —
And never can be sundered without tears."

The æsthetical ideal cannot be formulated; but that it possesses a certain constant and universal element receives convincing testimony from a general consensus of taste which is evidenced in the universal appreciation of certain forms of beauty, both in nature and in art. It must be acknowledged, to be sure, that there is an indefinite variety in taste; but in the midst of the bewildering chaos of conflicting appreciations there has formed a recognized ideal which in art we call classic. It is universally recognized, if not in detail, at least in the broad lines of its imperious commands.

This ideal may be regarded merely as a psychical phenomenon, the combined result of environment and of the schooling of the general taste through certain initial customs of criticism which originally set the drift in some one general direction. On the other hand, it may be urged that there is a metaphysical foundation underlying such an ideal in the sense of there being in nature manifestations of an absolute beauty, which accounts for its universal appreciation. It is to be noted in this connection that there is more substantial agreement concerning the beautiful in nature than the beautiful in art. The problem here is similar to that which was found so perplexing in the sphere of ethics, as to whether there is absolute, or only relative value in the ideal and the canons therein prescribed.

There is a further problem of æsthetics which is one of interest because of its bearings upon the more general problems of philosophy. It is this: "Does the æsthetic judgment, the appreciative consciousness, reveal a truer and deeper knowledge of nature than do the intellectual and moral judgments?" It is held that under quickened æsthetical sensibility we become conscious in a mystical manner of the spirit of nature which breathes and lives through all things; that especially the poets, in moments of rapt ecstasy, see visions and dream dreams which illumine the mystery of existence and withdraw apace the veil which conceals the vast unknown. Kant found in the æsthetical judgment a solution of the difficulties connected with the judgments of Pure Reason and the judgments of Practical Reason. For while the former are purely of intellectual origin and the latter compose that mass of moral truths which stand as law to the will, yet neither through the intellect nor through the will do we come to know the reality which underlies the phenomena of experience. Kant insists, therefore, that we are able to apprehend the real nature of the world of perception only through a bond of sympathy which is felt to exist between reality and our own souls in the appreciation of the beautiful; and that, therefore, our æsthetic judgments possess an element of universality, because they are the recognition of the universal reason in nature. This thought Matthew Arnold has expressed in substance where he asserts that "to see things in their beauty is to see things in their truth."

Closely akin to the appreciation of beauty is the recognition of the teleological or the purposeful in nature. It is an intuition of the order and harmony of the world, not only as beautiful, but as disclosing a profound plan and a vast design. The æsthetic sense, therefore, has that poetic, and likewise prophetic, insight which doubts not through the ages one increasing purpose runs. The mind that is keenly sensible of the existence and the import of ideals has more than a lively appreciation of their worth; such a mind can enter into the creative mind of the universe to the extent that it becomes itself creative, and in the various forms of art gives expression to that which is seen in waking dreams, and which is the "spirit and finer sense of all knowledge." Kant defines genius as the intelligence which works like nature. And according to Schelling the Absolute reveals Himself in the artist's creative work, disclosing the secrets of nature and the innermost nature of reality. It is thus by the æsthetic insight that man penetrates the surface show of phenomena, and discovers their essential significance in the spirit of reason, which, as beauty and purpose, is manifested in them. While this is substantially the conception of one of the most prevalent forms of modern idealism, it is a thought which is of ancient and honorable lineage; it may be traced to an early Greek origin. It is essentially Platonic; it finds expression also in the writings of Plotinus, who was imbued with Platonic ideas, and who regarded all beauty as the outshining of the inner spirit through the imprisoning shell of external matter.

In this connection, Hegel's conception of art must not be overlooked. He regards art as the triumph of mind over matter, because it impresses upon the phenomenal a "reality which is born of mind." While the living idea is thus embodied through sensuous media and forms, still all forms of art do not embody the idea in an equal degree of perfection. In architecture there is a dualism between mind and matter, inasmuch as the material does not satisfactorily express the idea but is rather a symbol which stands for the idea. In sculpture the idea is more adequately expressed through the material medium. It however is inferior to painting in this respect, because the soul of thought glances in the eye which in the statue is ever cold and inert. Music, being more subjective, is therefore more expressive of the inner moods and feelings. Poetry, however, is the art of arts; for the idea finds its most complete expression in words, and the material as vehicle of the thought is most thoroughly subordinate to the idea. In poetry, moreover, the blending of form and thought realizes an ideal synthesis of the subjective and objective. Throughout Hegel's conception of art, as thus outlined, it will be seen, therefore, that there is a creative function of the idea which produces the beauty of thought in a medium which is originally without form and void.

The æsthetical concept is regarded by Lotze, also, as a solvent of the difficulties which complicate the epistemological problem. He holds that reality is manifested in three ways, — as universal laws to which the real in its various aspects is necessarily subject; and as the real substances and forces which are the material content of things; and again as a plan according to which the manifold elements of the real are brought together in such a manner as to realize a specific end or idea. Lotze's contention is, that reason and conscience fail to discern that these three moments of reality are connected through any underlying unity, but that the cognizance of beauty pledges the existence of such a unity, dimly felt and vaguely conceived, yet satisfactory withal. Lotze's definition of beauty, therefore, is "the appearance to immediate intuition of a unity amongst those three powers (law, matter, and idea), which our cognition is unable completely to unite."[1]

There is still a further question of general interest, — the relation of æsthetics to ethics. There is a tendency among certain writers to identify the good and the beautiful. The ethical systems of Shaftesbury and Hutcheson are representative in an eminent degree of this general doctrine. This would be naturally expected and readily inferred from their appeal to a moral sense which is closely akin to the

[1] *Outlines of Æsthetics*, p. 11.

æsthetic sense, as the source whence all knowledge of moral distinctions emanates. Evil conduct thus proceeds from a deficient or abnormal taste, while right conduct is good taste. Schiller, with a half poetic and a half philosophic insight, has laid special stress upon the practical influence of æsthetic ideals upon the evolution of ethical concepts and conduct. He contends that man through contact with the beautiful is always infused with its refining spirit to the extent that he is thereby rendered less susceptible to the allurements of evil, and thus the will and desire are brought into harmony. Schopenhauer, who finds the essence of evil in the unrestrained strivings of the will, suggests that in the intuition of the beautiful, there is a benign influence which calms the fever of the will, and restores a normal self-poise. The ideal, according to Schiller, is the *Schöne Seele*, the " beautiful soul," which experiences no internal struggle between the behests of duty and the promptings of inclination, but in which the "play impulse," that exuberance of vitality, and overflow of spirit, instinctively realizes itself in the sphere of the good rather than the evil. It is the same idea which Wordsworth has expressed in his "Ode to Duty":—

> "Serene will be our days and bright,
> And happy will our nature be,
> When love is an unerring light
> And joy its own security."

There is here a tempering of the harsh rigorism of Kant, who insists that the very essence of morality lies in the inner struggle, the strenuous battling of the higher with the lower in our natures. The Kantian idea, however, must not be wholly overlooked in one's enthusiasm to construct an ethic along the lines of least resistance; for often through sensuous struggle a freedom of spirit is wrought. The idea of the æsthetic impulse towards the good is most suggestive if it be not constrained to embrace the whole range of ethical experience. It may be of some interest to trace this idea also to that ancient source, to which modern thought is under such obligation, and to find in Plato its most impressive expression: —

"'Right speech, then, and rightness of harmony and form and rhythm minister to goodness of nature; not that good-nature which we so call with a soft name, being really silliness, but the frame of mind which in very truth is rightly and fairly ordered in regard to the moral habit.'

"'Most certainly,' he said.

"'Must not these qualities, then, be everywhere pursued by the young men if they are to do each his own business?'

"'Pursued, certainly.'

"'Now painting, I suppose, is full of them [those qualities which are partly ethical, partly æsthetic], and all handicraft such as that; the weaver's art is full of them, and the inlayer's art, and the building of houses, and the working of all the other apparatus of life; moreover the nature of our own bodies, and of all other living things. For in all these, rightness or wrongness of form is inherent. And wrongness of form, and the lack of rhythm, the lack of harmony are fraternal to faultiness of mind and character; and the opposite qualities to the opposite condition, the temperate and good character: fraternal, aye! and copies of them.'

"'Yes, entirely so,' he said.

"'Must our poets, then, alone be under control, and compelled to work the image of the good into their poetic works, or not to work among us at all; or must the other craftsmen too be controlled and restrained from working this faultiness, and intemperance, and illiberality, and formlessness of character, whether into the image of living creatures, or the houses they build, or any other product of their craft whatever; or must he, who is unable so to do, be forbidden to practise his art among us, to the end that our guardians may not, nurtured in the images of vice as in a vicious pasture, cropping and culling much every day, little by little from many sources, composing together some one great evil in their own souls, go undetected? Must we not rather seek for those craftsmen who have the power, by way of their own natural virtue, to track out the nature of the beautiful and seemly, to the end that, living as in some wholesome place, the young men may receive good from every side, whencesoever, from fair works of art, either upon sight or upon hearing, anything may strike, as it were a breeze bearing health from kindly places, and from childhood straightway bring them unaware to likeness and friendship and harmony with fair reason?'"[1]

This passage has been quoted at length because it strikingly illustrates the old Greek virtue of καλοκἀγαθία, that æsthetic impulse towards the good, and because this idea has reappeared in so many forms in philosophy and in poetry alike. It appeals to the mind of the poet especially because there is a mystical element which characterizes the process of character development through the transmutation of the beautiful into the good. In Shelley's "Hymn to Intellectual Beauty" there is a rehabilitation of the old Platonic idea in one of its most exquisite expressions : —

[1] Plato, *Republic*, III. 401.

> "Spirit of Beauty, * * *
>   Thy light alone — like mist o'er mountains
>   driven,
>   Or music by the night wind sent,
>   Thro' strings of some still instrument,
>   Or moonlight on a midnight stream,
>   Gives grace and truth to life's unquiet dream.
> * * * * * * * *
>   Thus let thy power, which like the truth
>   Of nature on my passive youth
>   Descended, to my onward life supply
>   Its calm — to one who worships thee,
>   And every form containing thee,
>   Whom, SPIRIT fair, thy spells did bind
>   To fear himself, and love all human kind."

It must be observed again, however, that while fully recognizing the fraternal kinship of the good and the beautiful, nevertheless it does violence to the integrity of the ethical concept to derive its significance and force wholly from the æsthetic concept.

The intimate relation between these two concepts may be further unfolded through the consideration of the common characteristic which they possess, in that they each mirror the Eternal Spirit of the universe through kindred though different modes of manifestation. As Emerson says: "Truth and goodness and beauty are but different faces of the same All." It is by no means necessary to interpret Emerson's thought in a pantheistic sense. It commends itself especially to the theist. The intimations of divinity are revealed and yet half concealed in every form of beauty. They underlie the ancient Hebrew conception of the worship of God in the beauty of holiness, the beatific vision of Dante, the sovereign splendor of beauty in Plato's hierarchy of eternal forms, and Goethe's characterization of nature as the garment of the living God.

INDEX

Actualists 79 f.
Æsthetics 28, 31, 181 f.
Ahrens 166
Anarchy 178
Anaxagoras 61
Anaximander 59
Anaximenes 60
A posteriori 27, 97, 136, 163
A priori 27, 97, 131 f., 136, 160 f., 165
Aquinas, Thomas 172
Aristippus 145
Aristophanes 1
Aristotle 16, 78, 130, 158
Arnold 186
Art 181, 184, 188 f.
Association, Theory of 89 f.
Atheism 68
Atomism 33 f., 62, 63
Austin 167, 171, 173, 175

Bacon 2, 131
Bagehot 174
Balfour 10
Baumgarten 181
Beattie 109
Beauty, Philosophy of 181 f.
Begriff 120
Bentham 146, 147, 167
Berkeley 109

Bluntschli 168, **171**
Browning 56, 155
Büchner 47
Buddha 80
Butler 139

Cabanis 39, 46
Categorical imperative 146
Causation 43 f., 131 f.
Cicero 162, 165
Clarke 139
Comte 100 f., 157
Concept 119 f.
Conceptualism 124 f.
Condillac 97
Conscience 134 f.
Consciousness 44 f., 50
Conservation of energy 39 f.
Cosmology 18, 20 f., 30, 59 f.
Critical school, The 99
Cudworth 139
Cumberland 139
Cyrenaicism 145

Dante 172, 197
Deduction 130 f.
Deism 22, 65, 67
Democritus 33, 34, 35, 46, 49, 62, 63

INDEX

Descartes 35, 93, 99
Determinism 152
D'Holbach 46
Diderot 46
Dualism 19 f., 33

Edicts, The prætorian 164
Emerson 197
Empedocles 60, 61
Empiricism 26 f., 97 f., 131 f., 135 f., 160 f., 167
Epicurus 63, 146
Epistemology 24 f., 30, 95 f., 132 f., 189
Ethics 28 f., 31, 134 f., 160, 190 f.
Eudæmonism 148
Evolution, The theory of 44 f., 136 f., 149, 156, 169 f.

Fechner 54
Feuerbach 39, 47, 77
Fichte 9, 114 f.
Flint 47
Form of the ethical concept 141
Fouillée 170
Freedom of the will 152 f.

Geulincx 37
Gladstone 10
Goethe 4, 10, 68, 126, 182, 197
Green 91, 113, 144, 166, 177
Grotius 165

Haeckel 47
Hamilton 112
Hedonism 145 f.

Hegel 9, 77, 114 f., 143, 166, 170, 188
Hegelians of the Left 77
Helvétius 46
Heraclitus 60
Herbart 93, 117
Herbert, Lord 67
Herder 9, 115
Historical school of jurisprudence 171
History, The philosophy of 12
Hobbes 54, 146, 165, 167, 175
Holland 174
Homer 125
Hume 86 f., 99, 110, 167
Hutcheson 139, 190

Idealism 25 f., 109, 114 f., 170, 178
Identity, The theory of 38, 51 f.
Immanence, Divine 66, 71, 74
Indeterminism 153 f.
Individualism 178 f.
Induction 130 f.
Inference 119, 128 f.
Innate ideas 97 f.
Intellectual intuitionalism 139
Intellectualism 92 ff.
Intuitional theory of ethics 135 f., 155

James 83
Judgment 119, 126 f.
Jurisprudence 159 f.
Jus civile 162, 164

Jus gentium 164
Jus naturae 173
Jus naturale 162

Καλοκἀγαθία 195
Kant 81, 91, 99, 110 f., 115, 139, 140, 141, 153, 154, 163, 165, 166, 185, 186, 187, 192
Keats 1
Kipling 7
Knowledge, Relation of, to reality 101, 112
Krause 166

Laissez-faire policy 179
La Mettrie 46
Lange 46, 110
Law, Natural 162 f
Law, Positive 162
Law, The origin of 160 f.
Law, The science of 159 f.
Leibniz 34, 35, 36, 48, 49, 54, 93, 99
Lessing 10, 115
Locke 68, 95, 97, 99, 109, 175
Logic 28, 31, 118 f.
Lotze 3, 94, 189, 190

Macchiavelli 167, 168, 169, 172
McCosh 109
Maine 174
Malbranche 157
Martineau 69, 75, 86, 139, 156
Materialism 38 f., 61, 76, 77, 154, 178

Maurice 8
Mechanical explanation of the universe 21, 63
Metaphysics 17 f., 22, 23
Mill 5, 99, 147, 167
Mind 16, 78 f.
Mind and matter 38, 49, 53
Moleschott 47
Monads of Leibniz 34, 49
Monism 19 f., 33, 38, 49
Monotheism 65
Montesquieu 170
Morley 10

Naturalism 169 f.
Natural rights 175 f.
Natura naturans 75
Natura naturata 75
Nature 16, 185 f.
Neo-Spinozism 54
Normative sciences 28 f., 118

Occasionalism 37
Ontology 18 f., 22, 30, 32 f., 103
Oswald 109

Pantheism 22, 66, 68 f., 197
Parallelism 51 f.
Parmenides 61
Parsimony of causes 41
Pater 125
Paulsen 90
Percept 119
Perception 96, 102 f., 112, 119
Perfectionism 143
Personality 143 f., 177, 179 f.

Phenomenalism 110
Plato 5, 49, 104 f., 125, 157, 193 f., 195, 197
Plotinus 188
Pluralism 33 f.
Poetry, Relation to philosophy 6 f.
Politics, The science of 158 f.
Pollock 174
Polytheism 22, 64 f.
Positivism 99 f.
Potentia naturae 173
Preëstablished harmony 36 f.
Price 139
Protestantism and philosophy 9
Psychology 23 f., 29, 30, 78 f.
Psychology, Genetic 92
Puchta 171

Rationalism 27, 95 f.
Reaction theory 35 f.
Realism 25 f., 107 f.
Realism, Scholastic 122 f.
Reality 13 f., 101, 113, 121, 123, 127, 129, 183, 186, 189 f.
Reason 118 f.
Reid 109
Relativity of knowledge 112
Res cogitans 35
Res extensa 35
Reymond, Du Bois 58
Rigorism 140
Robertson 8

Romanes 55
Rousseau 165, 175

Savigny 171
Schelling 9, 114 f., 126, 187
Schiller 10, 191
Schopenhauer 49, 94, 191
Science, its relation to philosophy 5
Scottish philosophy 109, 113
Self, Nature of the 79 f., 154
Self-realization 143 f.
Sensationalism 97
Sentimental intuitionalism 139
Seth, Andrew 113
Shaftesbury 139, 190
Shelley 126, 195
Smith, Adam 139
Social-contract, The theory of 175 f.
Social factor in the ethical concept 151 f., 158 f.
Socialism 178 f.
Socrates 1
Sovereignty 171 f.
Spencer 54, 149
Spinoza 54, 74, 93, 99, 115, 157, 173
Spiritualism 38, 48 f., 61
State, The theory of the 159 f.
State control 177 f.
Stephen 151
Stewart 109
Stoics 140, 165
Substantialists 79
System, The world of knowledge regarded as a 129

Teleology 21, 72 f., 186 f
Tennyson 8
Thales 2, 59
Theism 22, 66 f., 155, 196 f.
Transcendence, Divine 66, 71
Transcendental theory of ethics 136 f., 142 f., 155
Trendelenburg 165

Universal relations 129 f.
Universals, The nature of 122 f.

Utilitarianism 136 f., 145 f. 156, 167 f.

Vogt 47
Voltaire 68
Voluntaryism 92 f.

Wallace 72
Windelband 63, 124
Wordsworth 69, 192
World regarded as eject 55

Xenophanes 60

www.ingramcontent.com/pod-product-compliance
Lightning Source LLC
Chambersburg PA
CBHW031819220426
43662CB00007B/712